The Self,
The Christ:
Individual,
Yet Collective!

This writing discusses who and what is our ultimate Self. The manuscripts' composition elaborates on the nature of the Self using Jungian Analytical Psychology terminology. Dozens of passages from the Holy Bible, particularly the Gospels and Paul's Epistles, are utilized to give credence to the title of this document. It also considers how the use of the word *Christ* is used and evolved within the span of the books of the Bible. This book also explores what are the Messianic Times, the Second Coming, the Atonement, and what a Collective Christ action might look like. This work also includes a view from modern science and from the Platonic philosophical tradition.

Julian Enoch Bruno, M.A.

A *Songs of Science* Book

ISBN: 1461022193
ISBN-13: 978-1461022190

Copyright Notice

Dedication

This book is dedicated to the realization of what Saint Paul writes in the Epistle to the Colossians of "the Christ in you, the hope of glory," and to the actualization of the Christ as Us, our destined glory, because all of humanity is waiting with earnest expectation for the unveiling manifestation of the Sons of God.

Table of Contents
*****

Acknowledgements

I would like to acknowledge all those men and women, saints as far as I my concerned, who have lead the way in their efforts at uncovering the nature of our True Self and the universe, such as those who I have quoted in this writing, and for sharing their discovery with humanity so that we all may live a Christ Conscious life.

I would like to thank Margaret D., who showed me much loving kindness and helped me with the initial writing of this material back in the 1990's.

I would like to thank Justine Boyer of Boyer Creative Graphic Design Firm for putting together the cover, both front and back, for this book.

Finally, I 'd like to acknowledge Huston Smith, the author of <u>The World's Religions</u>, who was the commencement speaker for our 2003 graduation class of Master's Degree in Consciousness Studies at the University of Philosophical Research. For he found it very fitting to instruct us on the money changers issue, with Jesus' action at the temple and how some of that issue has unfolded in the history of America, knowing that those who would take up the study of Consciousness, and have any concern for justice and the preservation of culture and of civilization would ultimately have to deal with this most central topic. Therefore, I have attempted to address this issue in my own way in Chapter 4.

A

Preface: Why I wrote this book

Simply put, I wrote this book to get clear on this topic: that the Christ is, among other things to be detailed more later, a Consciousness available to all, and as the Gospel of John (1:3-4) states, "All things came to be through him, and without him nothing came to be," and that our true, ultimate self is what is called in Christianity *the Christ*. I am not just talking about the historical person Jesus, but rather the power of the Logos beyond the manifestation of a personality through which all exist and are patterned.

As I was evolving in this teaching, this revelation, this unveiling, though still early on in the renewing of my mind with it, I thought I'd share the excitement and the joy of it with a friend. He didn't receive it well. His religious orientation was that even to read material other than the Bible was somehow wrong, and I don't believe I am exaggerating the situation. Well, his attitude turned out to be the motivation for me to know with certainty that what was initially shared, and what is contained in this document, is thoroughly supported Biblically (for those who need it) and is Truth beyond doubt.

With that stated, may the reader of this material find a perspective that will prove beneficial to you in your own quest for Truth, especially with regard to what we are, not just who we are. The material herein discussed is the reason why I left a traditional church – to find a more accurate, substantial, and a supportive view of humanity, which I found in Unity Church of Christianity. Please note, however, that this is not some official work of that church. I also find comfort in the Unitarian Universalist view, which states: "We believe in the freedom of religious expression. All individuals should be encouraged to develop their own personal theology, and to present openly their religious opinions without fear of censure or reprisal."

This work should not be considered as arrogant, but rather as one tenaciously affirming the truth of what we are. The idea is to take on the attitude of Jesus as depicted in four various locations in the Gospel of John:

> Amen, amen, I say to you, a son cannot do anything on his own, but only what he sees his father doing; for what he does, his son will do also (5:19).

> I cannot do anything on my own; I judge as I hear, and my judgment is just, because I do not seek my own will but the will of the one who sent me (5:30).

> My teaching is not my own but is from the one who sent me. Whoever chooses to do his will shall know whether my teaching is from God or whether I speak on my own. Whoever speaks on his own seeks his own glory, but whoever seeks the glory of the one who sent him is truthful, and there is no wrong in him (7:16-18).

> When you lift up the Son of Man, then you will realize that I AM, and that I do nothing on my own, but I say only what the Father taught me. The one who sent me is with me. He has not left me alone, because I always do what is pleasing to him (8:28).[1]

Basically, the attitude is of taking no credit for the work per se and having total reliance on God. Also, it's putting aside the ego, like Jesus did by overcoming his temptation by telling the devil, "get thee behind me, Satan; for it is written, thou shalt worship the lord, thy God, and him only shalt thou serve."[2] Therefore, let us lift up one another, let us get beyond the senses and see with the mind's eye that we are all the children of one loving, Heavenly Father.

Introduction

The main theme of this writing is on the relation between the Christ and the Self; the term self will often be qualified by one or other adjectives such as *true, real, higher*, or *ultimate*. Further, I discuss this relationship between our true or ultimate self (in contrast to a false or limited self - the ego) and God. The purpose of this work is to bring to one's awareness the unity, oneness, and similitude of this ultimate Self, Christ, and God. The further purpose is to familiarize oneself with the fact that the Christ, being more than just meaning the anointed one, is a Consciousness that is available to every human that comes into this world, and is not just confined to a one-time expression within the entire history of humanity, that of Jesus. There could be no incarnation without a consciousness preceding it. Awareness is the issue. If it is one's goal to "spend eternity in heaven", then having awareness or being aware that you are in heaven is the implied prerequisite. How else would you know you are there? To have awareness of something implies that you possess a more foundational consciousness. I will draw support for this writing from a number of resources.

Chapter 1 explores one of the collective works of Carl G. Jung, <u>Aion: The Researches into the Phenomenology of the Self</u>. The intent is to give evidence that our real self is whole, complete, at-one with God, indistinguishable from the God-image, is, in Christian terms, the Christ, and is individual and collective. I will utilize Jungian Analytical Psychology perspective as the framework for this writing. Now while Jung doesn't qualify the word *self* with an adjective as I have, which I have done to differentiate this Christed Self from our false self the ego self; I am doing so in part because based on conversations that I had with people in certain circles they want to make the ego out to be your self, therefore, I qualify the terms. I will then go over what are the Christ and the Logos. We will consider a writing from Manly P. Hall, his <u>The</u>

Mystical Christ, on what he has to say about the Logos and the Christ. A quote from A Course in Miracles is cited in this chapter. I conclude this chapter and cite in two other chapters from an anthology called Teachings of the Christian Mystics.

Chapter 2 begins with an extended quote from the book, Cosmic Consciousness: A Study in the Evolution of the Human Mind, by Richard Buck, M.D. Though most of this chapter focuses on Biblical passages because the Bible is seen and revered as the authoritative Word of God and thereby meaning Truth, therefore, I have entitled a subsection of this chapter *It's In The Holy Bible* to convey the fact that the thesis presented in this writing is right there in the Bible hidden in plain sight. Since the Bible is said to be an inspired text then I have used a number of Bibles because the particular passage being cited I found inspiring. Six different Bibles will be used throughout the course of this writing: The Catholic Study Bible, Holy Bible – From the Ancient Eastern Text which is George M. Lamsa's Translation, and The New Scofield Reference Bible – Holy Bible – Authorized King James Version will be main three bibles used. But I have also used The Complete Parallel Bible, which has four Bibles in it and I have used three of those within it: *The New Revised Standard Version*, *The New American Bible*, and also *The New Jerusalem Bible*. Many quotes from Jesus are used to support the theme of this writing. Also, Paul's epistles demonstrate and make clear that the Christ is a consciousness that is beyond the historical Jesus, is therefore collective and thereby not solely confined to one individual manifestation. That Christ is and expresses as your/our *ultimate self* is the ultimate message being conveyed in this writing. Lionel Corbett's book The Religious Function Of The Psyche, which offers a Depth Psychological approach, which is to say that it offers a spiritual approach to the psyche, will be featured. I will also explore the idea of "The Office of the Christ" which is found in the material The Book of Knowledge: The Keys of Enoch. Quotes from Paramahansa Yogananda's book, Autobiography of a Yogi, Dr. Rocco

Errico's book, <u>Let There Be Light: The Seven Keys</u>, and Donald Curtis' book, <u>Finding the Christ</u>, are also cited. And finally, two works by Edward Schillebeeckx, those being <u>Jesus: An Experiment in Christology</u> and <u>Christ: The Experience of Jesus as Lord</u>, will be included. By the name of their very titles these two books should give us some clue as to the reality with which we are concerned with, that being while Jesus was the Christ he is not solely it.

     Chapter 3 explores two works of the Church of Jesus Christ of Latter Day Saints, <u>The Book of Mormon</u> and <u>Doctrine and Covenants</u>. This chapter also considers a book on what's happening in science entitled, The<u> Field: The Quest for the Secret Force of the Universe</u>, by Lynn McTaggart.

     Chapter 4 is devoted to Erich Fromm's book, <u>You Shall Be As Gods</u>, and emphasizes "the messianic time" and what and who the "messiah" is and how he/she is going to come forth. And in a related matter we will explore the teaching of the Second Coming. The chapter also goes over what a Collective Christ action might look like, and also cites a quote from Franklin Roosevelt's inaugural address in 1933. And in this vein of a Collective Christ action a passage from <u>The Urantia Book</u> is reviewed. We also consider the philosopher Proclus' 13th Proposition of God being equated with the Good and the One. A statement from Abraham Maslow's The <u>Farther Reaches of Human Nature</u> will be brought to mind, as well as a few words from Buckminster Fuller on synergetics and being done with scarcity. The chapter wraps up with recalling the Preamble to the Constitution for the United States because, among a few other important things, it's about promoting the general welfare.

     A major objective is this work is to assert that, as an individual and collective body, we attune our attention away from a fragmentary view of ourselves and shift our thoughts toward viewing ourselves as whole and complete. In other words, we make a perceptual shift away from the idea that we are inherent sinners and onward toward the idea and fact that we are (humanity is) created in the image and similitude of God, are divine, worthy of the greatest good, and have an original blessing.   The point is, what one focuses their attention on grows, therefore, we have to view ourselves in a certain manner if we intend on bringing out our godliness.

I have quoted many texts in this document because the quotes used seemed to be one thought form being expressed, and therefore, felt no ego requirement to rephrase it such as if I originated the comment.   All the more I viewed it as if I was communing with other minds yet of One Mind, and it reminded me of Raphael's fresco paintings in the Stanza of the Signature at the Vatican, such as the School of Athens, Parnassus, or the Dispute on the Blessed Sacrament where even though the people represented weren't contemporaries, there is simultaneity of eternity where minds meet in unity. In the end I think what does show my originality is the overall construction of this book's compilation.

"Be On Guard"

At this point I'd like to address both those who object to this manuscript's title and its implication, and also any one in general who desires to comprehend some statements by Jesus that are the crux of the issue regarding this whole topic by citing some various scripture passages:

Mark 13, 21 reads, "If anyone says to you then, 'Look, here is the Messiah! Look, there he is!' do not believe it." [3] We have to keep in mind that when Jesus was addressing the people he was immediately talking to, it was people who viewed the messiah – *masiah* - or the Christ in military terms; that some military victor would come to the aid of Israel and save them and kick the Romans out. But Jesus was not going for this militant view that some Messiah/Christ would come save Israel militarily from Roman rule, so no, one wasn't to or shouldn't believe in a military savior. And, as an aside, if it just so happens that a George Washington or a Sam Houston turns out to be such type heroes', to save a people from imperial rule, one could sure be glad about it.

I would like to interject now a passage from Dr Rocco Errico, a minister who teaches Aramaic, who explains in his audio-cassette tapes, *Jesus Before Christianity* states:

> Did I explain messiah? This is very important that you understand this from its Jewish point of view and not our metaphysical or Christian (Church doctrine) point of view... It had nothing to do with divinity. How did we get all these interpretations from Christ? What influenced Christianity were the apocryphal books and scrolls which were in existence, which interpreted the messiah as a super-natural being, which crept into our Christian teachings in the church. This is how the Christology began to develop. We have a Christology of our own; those in New Thought call it Christ Consciousness, the Christ in you. It also developed under Paul; he talks about Christ in you, your hope of glory... We developed a Christology of our own, but originally it simply meant an anointed man. You had to be anointed to perform certain tasks. If you were going to lead the people of Israel, you had to be anointed by the priests.[4]

As Dr. Errico makes clear two thousand years later, the idea of the Christ, definition wise, has evolved beyond this strict meaning, which Paul's epistles goes a long way in evolving and which will be laid out in this paper. Today, we are not concerned with militarily saving Israel from Roman rule, and Jesus' statement has to be viewed as confined to a military situation, so sure don't believe in some misguided messianic hope to save Jerusalem from Roman destruction; or to generalize it for us today, save any city from some imperial destruction militarily, but if it comes to such battles it would be great to defeat such empire/imperial forces. That question Jesus himself surely had to consider, yet what would be the best way for that to happen? His approach was going to take a much longer range plan. Now to get back to the main theme, therefore, Jesus' use of the word is not the same as Paul's use of the word as we shall see. So no, I am not advocating being a messiah or a Christ militarily speaking, yet Jesus' enterprising plan would certainly generate those first centuries of saints that did, in their own way, help put an end to an empire. Therefore, I am affirming to be a Christ as Paul has used the term, and if it means in some mysterious, long term millennial plan means putting an end to imperialism and empire as those first tier of Christian saints did, then I accept my part in that meaning. So with that said here's another quote:

> When some of the Pharisees asked Jesus when the kingdom of God would come, he answered, saying to them, The kingdom of God does not come by observation. Neither will they say, Behold, it is here, Or behold, it is there! **For, behold, the Kingdom of God is within you.**[5] (Emphasis added).

What, the <u>kingdom of God is within you</u>?! If anyone does tell you, 'Look, the Messiah is here or there,' you should question it because the whole idea is to realize that we are the Kingdom of God, "the body of Christ," as Paul writes. So, we don't go follow any so-called messiah because **we each have our own inner God/Christ appointed and directed path to live,** and yet there is a collective Christhood to be developed too since we are all the body of Christ. Further, if and since God is Love, then we have to consider ourselves amongst the chosen. My efforts here are not to impersonate Jesus or diminish his efforts, and I am here to tenaciously acknowledge the fact that the kingdom of God is within just as Jesus taught; therefore, we don't have to look for any external messiah. And since the Kingdom is within or is at hand, then it is our responsibility to seek first the kingdom of God so as to obtain His/Her counsel to know the right use of all things. Therefore, please truthfully consider the theme postulated in this book. Remember, we have been given the Mind of Christ.

Now when it comes to comprehending that the kingdom of God doesn't come by observation, which has to be understood as not coming by logical positivists, reductionism, or British empiricism of sense certainty, rather the kingdom of heaven comes when one opens their mind to comprehend and cognize what is and how the Logos operates.

Another few scriptures are, Luke 21:8, 19: "He answered, 'See that you not be deceived, for many will come in my name, saying, 'I am he,' and 'The time has come.' Do not follow them! [...] By your perseverance you will secure your lives."[6] Matthew 24 and Mark 13 have similar content, but the point here is that notes from this study bible for Luke 21: 8 instruct that "the proclamation of the imminent end of the age has itself become a false teaching."[7] And while ages do end eventually and a next age begins, it is also important to point out that the New Scofield Reference Bible, Authorized Version has Luke 21: 19 read as, "In your patience possess ye your souls." Or even as the Lamsa Bible reads this verse, "By your patience you will gain your souls."

Doesn't it just make you wonder? What's this verse saying? **You will save your lives (self)?!** You mean Jesus doesn't do that for you? Jesus isn't going to descend upon a cloud and rapture us? If anything is going to descend upon you, it will be the consciousness of the Christ Mind to raise your awareness of your role within the Body of Christ, and to establish the Kingdom of Heaven on earth. The point is that while God the Father, Jesus, and the Holy Spirit each have their divine part in saving souls and there are scriptures that support such, humanity too has its part to play and this writing addresses our part in the whole equation.

It would be useful for those who oppose this perspective to consider all the other references that support the Self/Christ theme that runs through the Bible. Afterwards, I welcome a rational, reasonable rebuttal, without resort to name calling, condemnation and judgment. The thing that I find so remarkable is this: I am affirming and this document supports that we are created in the image and likeness/similitude of God, that God is All in All, that Christ is everything in all of you, and that we are the body of Christ, **then and therefore**, at some level, which includes this realm, we are IT - God expresses as us and we cannot be separate from God. Christ is you, is me, and is everyone. Yes, I'm saying that we are an aspect of God; the answer is explicitly stated right in the very book people are asserting where it is to find truth. Ultimately the Bible is but an artifact, which only points to the kingdom, which is within us and is us; and it is for us to look out upon the world from the divine-kingdom within because that's where we are coming from and then participate in the building of heaven on earth. So if a certain segment of Christians can't quite accept their own Christhood yet, its okay, eventually they will get it. Because the idea is to embrace the Atonement, which is better understood as the At-one-ment, which is a glimpse into eternity, oh, my brothers and sisters do you see the affinity and the equality between you and me. For some this happened simultaneously, for the rest it occurs successively, however the order, it's certainly about having everyone be present.

If you have already accepted Jesus Christ, then how about putting on the mind of Christ? Jesus is asserting that <u>the kingdom of God is within you</u> and by patient endurance you will save your lives. Therefore, "be on guard" against those who would have you be a wretch, against those that would keep you fragmented and/or flawed; against those that say you can never escape sin; against those who would teach that God is only in some far-off remote location external to you, and thereby deny your real, true, ultimate self. Remember it is this ultimate self of yours that is created in the image and similitude of that which we call God or YHWH (and the various permutations of His/Her name takes), and St. Paul throughout his epistles calls this Self the Christ, so therefore, remember what the Creator and the Holy Spirit would have you be – coherent, whole, and complete - and what to do.

Chapter 1

Jungian Analytical Psychology Perspective

I will begin reference support for this writing with Jungian Analytical Psychology. From this view the focus of attention is on the individual's psyche, and on the person's inner experience. It also concerns itself with balance – that is to be and have an integrated personality of both the inner subjective world and the outer empirical world – to be whole. In Analytical Psychology the personality of the individual consists of four aspects: the ego, the shadow, the anima or animus, and the self. The *self* aspect of the personality will be the focus of this writing. Quotes from Dr. Jung's writings in this book will come from <u>Aion: The Researches into the Phenomenology of the Self</u>, mainly chapters IV and V.

The Self

The self is the total personality, which encompasses the other aspects of the personality (outlined in the next section). The self consists of both the conscious and the unconscious parts of the personality. The self is all that there is. "Unity and wholeness" is what the self represents in all people.[8]

It is a normal/natural human tendency to view oneself as whole and complete because our true created being is such. Thereby attempts on the part of religious hierarchical, "churchianity" structures to make us out to be different (inherently flawed or original sinners), or that we come into the world as a "blank slate" taught by empires, with their *empir-cism*, are to be rejected.   To apply meaning to experiences that makes one feel whole and complete or to seek out such experiences that would make one feel as such is the order of the day. And Life is ever moving in the direction so as to achieve and/or maintain wholeness and completion; and in realizing this perception of completion the self is, in a fashion, "perfect". It is to and for the experience of these living ideals that I do this writing: to experience wholeness and unity, to feel complete, and to be certain of the ideals' objectivity, and to outright declare it so is what the Self engages in and promotes. To maintain their extension in time is the goal of the self. The duty of the self is to integrate all the other aspects of the personality. As Jung puts it:

> Unity and totality stand at the highest point on the scale of objective values because their symbols can no longer be distinguished from the *imago Dei*. Hence all statements about the God-image apply also to the empirical symbols of totality. Experience shows that individual mandalas are symbols of *order*, and that they occur in patients principally during times of psychic disorientation or re-orientation. As magic circles they bind and subdue the lawless powers belonging to the world of darkness, and depict or create an order that transforms the chaos into a cosmos. The mandala at first comes into the conscious mind as an unimpressive point or dot, and a great deal of hard and painstaking work as well as the integration of many projections are generally required before the full range of the symbol can be anything like completely understood. If this insight were purely intellectual it could be achieved without much difficulty, for the world-wide pronouncements about the God within us and above us, about Christ and the *corpus mysticum*, [...] are all formulations that can easily be mastered by the philosophic intellect. This is the common source of the illusion that one is then in possession of the thing itself. But actually one has acquired nothing more than its name, despite the age-old prejudice that the name magically represents the thing, and that it is sufficient to pronounce the name in order to posit the thing's existence...
> [...] In psychology one possesses nothing unless one has experienced it in reality. Hence a purely intellectual insight is not enough, because one knows only the words and not the substance of the thing from inside.[9]

Some readers will come to this writing and find this

information new and provide for them the first intellectual insight to what their true self is, thereby, setting them on their path of individualization, of Self realization and Self actualization; others will reject it due to parental and religious conditioning yet the fact remains that this true Christ Self awaits for their acceptance, still yet others will come to this writing after having the substantiative numinous experience that provided them with the knowing that God is within and that they are at-one with God, and this writing will offer them some terminology they may not otherwise be utilizing.

So one of the first orders of business in this writing has been to acknowledge the Kingdom or the Christ within, as was done in the Preface, and while that is only the beginning it is a necessary step in the complete unfolding of the individuation/spiritual process. Saying that our ultimate self is the Christ is the message that is being conveyed here, but it doesn't mean that we have experienced that reality yet in this life but that is the objective; our ultimate objective is to have the numinous experience or experiences that provides us with the absolute knowing that we have in fact put on the Mind of Christ and have experienced that Presence that gives us certainty. Then from that point onward we are to live a life of service to humanity because the more people that realize their innate Godliness the better off everyone will be.

As Jung states, "The self is a God-image, or at least cannot be distinguished from one;"[10] this is exactly what the Holy Bible, the Book of Genesis, chapter 1:27 speaks of: "God created man in his image; in the divine image he created him; male and female he created them."[11] This is what all truth teachers teach – to Know Thyself – for he who knows him/herself knows God. While the Old Testament describes our self as being created in the image and similitude of God, the New Testament, especially Paul's Epistles, uses the word *the Christ in you*; this is essentially the same thing but with two different words. The Penguin Dictionary of Psychology has as the sixth definition of the word *self* thus:

> Self as abstract goal or end point on some personalistic
> dimension. This meaning is embodied specifically in the
> later writings of Jung, in which self became conceptualized
> as the ultimate archetype lying between consciousness and
> the unconscious, the achievement of self thus being the
> final human expression of spiritualistic development.[12]

It's no stretch at all then to conclude that if the Self is the
ultimate archetype of spiritualistic development then that
would be in Christian religious terms *the Christ*, and that is
what we are to develop and it begins by first accepting it and
taking it on.

The Other Aspects of the Personality

The definitions of the other aspects of the personality
are included so as to gain an understanding:

a) ego – the center of the field of consciousness. It is
the complex factor to which all conscious contents are related.
It is the subject of all personal acts of consciousness. It is the
person's conscious personality; therefore, all those features
that are unknown or unconscious to the subject are missing.
This is why the ego would be considered a *false self* because
you are more than just an ego.

b) shadow - to become aware of the shadow involves
recognizing the dark aspects of the personality as present and
real. The dark characteristics, that is, the inferiorities
constituting the shadow reveal that they have an emotional
nature, a kind of autonomy, and thereby an obsessive, even a
possessive quality. Its roots are in the unconscious. In
theological terms the shadow would be called the devil.

c) anima or animus (the syzygy) – the opposite gender
aspects of the personality, also having its roots in the
unconscious. The anima is feminine psychological tendencies
of men, while the animus is a female's masculine

psychological tendencies. Gender manifests on all planes; everything has its masculine and feminine principles.

An Archetype – Image and Appearance

An archetype is an original pattern, a prototype, or an original model from which duplicates are made. Jung writes "the archetypal image of wholeness, which appears so frequently in the products of the unconscious, has its forerunners in history."[13] What is being pointed out is the relation between the traditional Christ figure, Jesus, and the natural symbol of wholeness, the self, with symbols representing a certain kind of equality. Symbols can represent equality because we are speaking of being created in the image and similitude of God, this is an inner reality, a pattern that waits to be implemented. So to make known the resemblance between the Christ and the self, Jung adds to the "many symbolical amplifications of the Christ-figure yet another, the psychological one, or even so it might seem, reduce the Christ-symbol to a psychological image of wholeness." [14] Jung informs his readers that he is "not making a confession of faith or writing a tendentious tract, but simply considering how certain things could be understood from the standpoint of our modern consciousness."[15]

But I am making a confession of faith and writing for a cause, and that statement of faith is that we are being awakened to the idea and fact that our self, in some ultimate or true sense, is a sanctified, ideal figure who becomes Israel (he or she who contends with God until victory) and restores, not necessarily some modern nation-state in southwest Asia, but "a people who would have a higher 'perceptual channel' of spiritual energy connected with the power of the Shekinah/Holy Spirit."[16] Furthermore, let's consider the physical, bodily manifestation of Jesus the Christ as if we were looking into a mirror, and we recognized that the image we saw as our self, acknowledging its psychological origin, i.e., an internal locus of control. The self is spirit and is whole; this is, in fact, the Word made flesh. Therefore, as Jung proclaims, "the self proves to be the vision behind the supreme ideas of unity and totality that are inherent in all monotheistic and monistic systems."[17] This is what we are: our ultimate self expresses as the supreme personality, possessing the I Am That I Am consciousness. Humanity, as a whole, is not only realizing this truth of what we are, it is also actualizing this truth as well. And I affirm that humanity will collectively exemplify our unity, saving ourselves, civilization, and our planet, and that we are doing so even now.

The Christ

Now to determine what is the *Christ*? The Catholic Study Bible (CSB) defines the word *Christ* as:

> the Greek word for the Hebrew *masiah* (see messiah). Both words mean anointed, that is blessed by having oil poured over the head. By applying this title to Jesus, the early Christians expressed their belief that he was the messiah of Israel.[18]

Let's also define the word *messiah*; the CSB cites it as:

> Hebrew for "anointed." It could be applied to various officials, including priests, but came to refer especially to the king who was descended from David. (As part of the ritual when a king was enthroned, his head was anointed with oil.) In the period after the Exile, when there was no longer a king in Judah, the "messiah" came to mean an ideal figure that would restore the kingdom of Israel in the future.[19]

So the *Christ* is the "anointed one" and is a title; furthermore, it was not as if Jesus' last name was *Christ*. The situation would be more like *Jesus the Christ*, a title that would not be solely confined to him. For certainly the way Paul uses the word it takes on an expanded meaning, as we shall see. As one can see the meaning of the word evolved over the span of time that the books of the Bible were written, such as by how Paul uses the word *Christ* in his epistles, such as Col 1: 27, "the Christ in you, the hope of glory," which we will review later. Today, in certain circles, the word *Christ* seems to be connoted with the phrase "the only begotten Son of God" (to be discussed more later), and many attempt to make this statement apply only to Jesus. However, it is the premise or thesis of this writing that these descriptions do not exclusively apply to Jesus, so this book is in the vein of building a Christology, which includes you and I as an aspect of the meaning of the words Christ or Son (Daughter) of God. Implied in the meaning of this premise is the requirement of awareness, the awareness of a Christ Consciousness, if you will. This only begotten Christ Consciousness is available to every human being that comes into the world, and whoever did accept him he gave power to become children of God, just as the first chapter of the Gospel of John states. Therefore, it is the view of this author that "the Christ" expresses itself more infinitely throughout creation, and is not just attainable by the one expression – Jesus – throughout the whole history of humanity. This idea is not new, nor is it just the idea of this author, the rest of this writing will be devoted to showing various other writings and authors that point to us as included in this Sonship or Christed Being reality.

So to cite another author, in what I have seen as the most precisely stated comment on the differentiation of Jesus and the Christ, Manly P. Hall has put it the best:

> […] It is strange and wonderful that it should be Paul, who had never known Jesus the man, who alone understood the mystery of the Christ. That he did understand, we know from his words: "If any man is in Christ he is a new creation." We cannot read the words of Paul without realizing that the Christ whom he preached was not the Jesus of the Gospels but the Christos, the

anointed One, who was associated with Jesus at the time of the baptizing by John. For the years of the ministry, the Son of God and the son of man were united in one appearance, but at the time of the crucifixion they separated again. In spite of the specific teachings of Jesus, the disciples were not aware of the qualitative difference between a personal redeemer and a universal Saviour. It was the ministry of Paul which rescued the Christian faith from the limitations of time and locality. He made possible universal faith universally demonstrable. Had this not occurred, we should worship the history and not the mystery of Jesus.

Paul unfolded the Messianic tradition of the orthodox Jews by applying to it the Greek key to the mystery of the Logos. God is one eternal principle containing within itself all attributes and potencies.[20]

The Logos

Let's also consider the Greek version of the Gospel of John opening with a phrase "ho Logos", which in the English is "the Word", and Jesus the Christ is said to be the Word made flesh or the Logos. But what is the **Logos**? The Logos is much like an archetype, being a pre-existing Divine Blueprint, which implies Intelligence; yet it also means a manifestation/incarnation into (and even as) the material world. To say it another way, before anything manifested, there was a desire, a Divine Thought form, Logos, which was the creative source and then from the Pattern or Divine blueprint, Logos (as Demiurge) called forth and then emanated out as the material world, which was the in-stroke and out-stroke of creation. Other descriptive terms for the Logos are "proportion", in a technical sense "measure" or "reckoning", and "the unifying formula or proportionate method of arrangement of things."[21] These authors also have this to say about Logos:

> The effect of arrangement according to a common plan
> or measure is that all things, although apparently plural

and totally discrete, are really united in a coherent complex of which men themselves are a part, and the comprehension of which is therefore logically necessary for the adequate enactment of their own lives.[22]

Now how beautiful is that? One of the Presocratic philosophers, Heraclitus taught, five hundred years before Jesus was born, "Listening not to me but to the Logos it is wise to agree that all things are one."[23] Certainly the realm of the senses can lead one to think that there are many unrelated things, therefore, would you not agree that there is no way to ascertain that all things are one unless the senses are guided by the Mind? If Mind is present throughout the universe then one can "see" beyond sense capacity by confronting sensorial or ontological paradoxes through putting forth a hypothesis, then experimentally validating it and/or with someone else replicating the original discovery. While Logos is transcendent, the mind being the bridge between the worlds, creates immanent proofs by applying meaning to phenomena, and as a result we have a cosmology that is not dual or two but one, hence we have a universe.

The use of the word Logos is not confined only to Jesus the Christ as many Christians attempt to make it out to be, but the Logos is common to all and includes all of humanity, all of humanity shares in the quality of being that Jesus does - of being a creator. It is particularly worth noting and relevant to this writing Jesus' own words - and Heraclitus is telling us to listen to the Logos because this Intelligence is teaching us that all are one - John 17:20-23a reads:

> I pray not only for them, but also for those who will believe in me through their word, so that they may all be one, as you, Father, are in me and I in you, that they also may be in us, that the world may believe that you sent me. And I have given them the glory you gave me, so that they may be one, as we are one, I in them and you in me, that they may be brought to perfection as one. [24]

How plain is that? This one quote by Jesus alone should make it abundantly clear that we share equality. Does it not?

This is exactly what the Logos, as Jesus, reminds us of: that we are "one" as the Gospel of John relays, that we are an analog of the One, created in the image and similitude of YHVH. So here is a Greek Philosopher, circa 500 B.C. teaching about the Logos, which was commonly available to all people if they would but pay attention, be mindful and not just be confined to one's senses, but rather display some mental capacities to comprehend unity. Now he, Heraclitus, is not just talking about Jesus, but rather a cosmic Intelligence that readily reveals itself to those who are attentive. Achieving Oneness or union is contingent upon each of us availing ourselves to listening to the teachings of the Logos, period.

Therefore, it is the thesis of this paper that the two descriptions of "the Christ" and "the Father's only son" (from John 1: 14) are not a description confined exclusively to Jesus, but rather are just part of building a theology of Christology, which Paul himself develops in his epistles. This Christ/Logos Consciousness is available to all and "to those who did accept him he gave power to become children of God, to those who believe in his name" (John 1: 12). What does John 1: 3-4 say: "All things came to be through him, and without him nothing came to be. What came to be through him was life, and this life was the light of the human race." Therefore, it is also the view of this author that the Christ/Logos expresses itself infinitely throughout creation, and is not just attainable by the one expression, Jesus, throughout human history. The Christ/Logos is the power and Jesus is the pattern. Furthermore, it is to be explicated that we each attain an Anointing/Sanctification not so much today to restore the State of Israel, but it is bestowed upon us when we act as Jesus would and we put on the mind of Christ, and in some general way be an ideal figure to make restoration to and to improve this realm. Our objective, one among many, is to open ourselves to the awareness of this

Consciousness, a Consciousness of the Christ/Logos, that we may be "perfected" due to our attentiveness.

The Psychology of the Personality

At this point a bit more information has to be communicated about the psychology of the personality. Analytical teaching is that the "psychology of the personality has a twofold division: an 'extra-conscious' psyche whose contents are personal, and an 'extra-conscious' psyche whose contents are impersonal and collective."[25] The contents of this personal extra-conscious are acquired during the individual's lifetime, neither of these psyches are beyond conscious awareness in any absolute sense; that is, we have access to their contents. The impersonal and collective psyche "forms as it were an omnipresent, unchanging, and everywhere identical quality of the psyche per se."[26] The contents of this "collective unconscious" are of an archetypical nature that was "present from the beginning." [27]

I take two different directions at this point with Jung's work. First, the contents of this collective unconscious were present from the beginning of what? The beginning of creation? Yes, this is the case. For we have access to a Consciousness that was present at the beginning of creation, a Superconsciousness that is an aspect of our Self. We can become conscious of the contents of this collective unconscious in various ways: (1) by taking note of our dreams, (2) through vivid imaginations, (3) through inference by mythological motifs, (4) through mandalas, and (5) through the practice of meditation. For as the beginning of the Gospel of John has it, "In the beginning was the word, the word was in God's presence, and the word was God." Jesus said it thus, "Before Abraham was I Am" (John 8:58). This is the pre-existing Logos of which we are at one with. Our "extra-conscious" Self has been around, present, even alive if you will since the beginning of creation. Our Ultimate Self is the Word made flesh. We have access to this knowledge, to this Knowing, as well as to all knowledge because of what we are, "for there is nothing that is concealed that will not be revealed, and nothing hidden that will not become known," just as the Gospels of Matt. 10 and Luke. 8 proclaim.

The second direction that we will examine concerning the omnipresent, unchanging, and everywhere identical quality of this impersonal and collective extra-conscious psyche centers on psychic processes generally. As Jung writes, "...psychic processes in all individuals must be based on an equally general and impersonal principle that conforms to law, just as the instinct manifesting itself in the individual is only the partial manifestation of an instinctual substrate common to all men."[28] What is being stated here is an outright proclamation that what one person has experienced and achieved, all people can experience and achieve. Unity, wholeness, transfiguration, cellular regeneration, resurrection, atonement, and salvation - yes, we will achieve those very things our elder brother Jesus did and we are doing so even now because this is the Logos pattern. With this principle as law clearly in mind, Jung continues:

> This amounts to saying that in unconscious humanity there is a latent seed that corresponds to the prototype Jesus. Just as the man Jesus became conscious only through the light that emanated from the higher Christ and separated the natures in him, so the seed in unconscious humanity is awakened by the light emanating from Jesus, and is thereby impelled to similar discrimination of opposites.[29]

Jesus is the "prototype for the awakening of the third sonship slumbering in the darkness of humanity," because he awakened the divine seed that all human beings contain.[30] By certain practices we can then reflect light as a diamond or radiate with a halo like glow as saints do, and thus we look upon ourselves as beings of light; remember scripture has it that "you are the light of the world." While we are in the world we are to be bearers of light and truth.

A Threefold Sonship

Two questions that may arise upon the citing of these last quotes are: What is the nature of the "third sonship slumbering in the darkness of humanity," and what are the "opposites" that the rest of humanity is impelled to discern?

First, God begot a threefold sonship. The nature of the first son was the finest and subtlest, and thereby remained up above with the Father. The second son's nature was a bit grosser and descended a bit lower, but was capable enough to lift its heaviness up to the higher regions. The third son is said to be "the grossest and heaviest because of its impurity," therefore its "nature needed purifying." [31] These three aspects correspond to spirit, soul, and body respectively. Spirit and soul are stated to be, "of a subtle nature and dwell, like the ether and the eagle, in or near the region of light, whereas the body, being heavy, dark...but nevertheless contains the divine seed of the third sonship."[32] It must also be pointed out that the **Christ** is the name given to the first sonship *spirit* and the second sonship *soul*, while the third sonship, the *body*, is referred to as **Jesus, the son of Mary.**

Yet, while the body is referred to as impure, it contains the divine seed. For in the body, that is physical matter, is "lodged a third of the revealed Godhead;" therefore this body is significant, and it truly does make a difference.[33] We are divine beings, not just mere humans as so commonly cited. Humanity is important. Again I repeat, we are the Word made flesh, the incarnate Logos, being at-one with God, never separate. Now Jesus, the son of Mary, corresponds to the third sonship for he awakened this divine seed; therefore he was "purified and made capable of ascension by virtue of the fact that the opposites were separated in him through the Passion (i.e., through his division into four)."[34] And so the opposites became conscious.

A Discrimination of Opposites

Second, what opposites have to be discerned that we ourselves may awaken, be purified, and ascend as Jesus did? For, after all, we too are compelled to a similar discernment of the opposites being a part of the revealed Godhead; moreover, in essence, we are in containment of the complete trichotomy (spirit, soul, body), as Jesus. In potential, we have the same capacity as Jesus, with it being our mission here on earth to exemplify that wholeness as Jesus did.

The opposites are good and evil, and spiritual and material. On the psychological level these opposites are unified because of the fact that the self isn't solely good and spiritual, which makes the shadow not as dark. It is on this mind level that a dual between forces of good and evil is taking place; however, it is our duty to look beyond this seeming battle of forces, to see past the duality of the mind and the multiplicity of the body, to envision the reality of the One and Only Force that is present and active in the universe, and to look into the inner altar where all is one. The point is, we are spirit and it is here where we get our strength so it is important to be cognizant so as to maintain communication with the God Logos Intelligence; so, yes, we turn inward to ask the Logos Intelligence what is what regarding the opposites and then stay tuned to find Life's answers.

The self has the attributes of uniqueness and occurring only once in time, yet remember the self is the total personality, conveying the fullness of conscious and unconscious contents, therefore, another pair of opposites deals more directly with time and space than with perception of what is, as do the previous sets mentioned. With this being the case, the psychological self must be described in paradoxical terms due to its transcendent nature; that is, uniqueness and unitemporalness must be complemented with their opposites so that the "transcendental situation" can be correctly characterized. The opposite of unique is universal, while the opposite of unitemporal is eternal. Jung writes:

> This formula expresses not only the psychological self but also the dogmatic figure of the Christ. As historical personage Christ is unitemporal and unique; as God, universal and eternal. Likewise, the [S]elf; as the essence of individuality it is unitemporal and unique; as an archetypal symbol it is a God-image and therefore universal and eternal. [35]

And so it is by this truth that we are at-one with the omnipresent Life-Force we call God, never separate, with our true identity being spirit, yet not excluding physical matter either because we have a threefold nature.

Transcendence

What then is the transcendental situation? The transcendental situation is that the Self is conscious and yet has Superconsciousness. How can transcendence occur that we may ascend? It is by withholding judgment on what we perceive to be "good" or "evil", or "spiritual" or "materialistic", in that relative point in time after which we then call upon the Holy Spirit to reveal to us what is the truth, so that proper, Just Judgment will be achieved. This is the goal of the Self, to bring together the opposites, to integrate them, realizing that they are opposite ends of a spectrum or continuum. This is the Principle of Polarity, which states that everything is dual; everything has poles; everything has its pair of opposites; like and unlike are the same; opposites are identical in nature, but different in degree; extremes meet; all truths are but half-truths; all paradoxes may be reconciled.

Withholding of judgment can also be referred to as the stopping of projections, which is a defense mechanism in which a human attributes his or her undesirable characteristics onto another. In this withholding of judgment we go beyond the opposites to a new reality, a blending of the power of the two opposites so that we see the other person as our very self and see that our interests are inherently the same. Instead of calling it a new reality, the situation should be stated as, "the restoration of an original condition and not an alteration of consciousness."[36]   Because judgment is withheld and the Holy Spirit invited in, our vision is completely recalled to memory and our oneness with the God-image restored. It is in/with this that our minds are renewed and thereby we are transformed to prove what the will of God is, and we are not conformed to the thinking of the world because we ultimately acknowledge a creation centered cosmology.

The Vision

The vision that is restored to us is that we are the Christ of God, the only begotten Son which expresses itself infinitely throughout creation, our very True Self. We, as the whole of humanity, are truly divine expressions of the One. Our unitemporal and unique, yet eternal and universal Self expresses as God's holy Son or Daughter. And in each of our own process of individuation we will actualize the realization of our Christhood and are doing so even now. In our awareness we are conscious of the truth that we are no longer fallen, no longer separate from God, no longer original sinners. For we are At-one with the One, the Creator and the created being inseparable, containing an original blessing. This is truly glorious and outright cause for cheer.

We now know that the kingdom of God is within us, that the kingdom IS, and expresses AS us. Sit very still and know that you possess the I Am Consciousness. Our vital life force can be channeled upward, so that expanded degrees of consciousness can be awakened, as can be accomplished by the practice of meditation. The mystics throughout the ages and now men of science have recommended daily meditation and quiet time, here's a passage from Psalms:

> Blessed is the man who walks not in the way of the ungodly, nor abides by the counsel of sinners, nor sits in the company of mockers. But his delight is in the law of the Lord; and **on his law does he meditate day and night.** And he shall be like a tree planted by a stream of water, that brings forth its fruit in its season, whose leaves fall not off; and whatsoever he begins he accomplishes.[37] [Emphasis added.]

In the science realm an experiment was performed by Andrew Newberg, M.D., with Tibetan Buddhists meditating and with Franciscan nuns praying. Using research techniques that use radioactive tracers in the brains of the test subjects while they were having a "mystical experience" found that the neurons in the orientation association area of the superior parietal lobe "go quiet during these periods of intense focus and concentration."[38] This is the area of the brain that locates us in time and space; with this area silenced people experience a sense of 'oneness' with the universe. With the boundary between ourself, others, and the environment blurring; with time, space and even our sense of the ego self suspended a larger sense of self perceives as "endless and intimately interwoven with everyone and everything."[39]

The center between the brows is referred to by many names, the Third Eye for instance, but regardless, the idea is to experience the Absolute Reality of God and Your Ultimate Self. Be still, with eyes closed, and with concentration gaze on the spot directly between the brows of the eyes, just be. Beneficial results are forthcoming, even physiologically. Eternal life can be realized and experienced now, even while we are in our time and space suit (our body), due to our inherent connection with Life. The Infinite Knowledge of the One and Only Power has not been thwarted, this knowing is available now, experience these truths for yourself now.

The complete recalling to memory of our Atonement (At-one) with the Creator God must proceed by recognizing the face of Christ. Only by becoming conscious of that which is whole can the memory of God return. The beauty of all this is that to recognize means to know again. It is awareness that Something Real and Valid from before is perceived a second time, indicating that this knowledge is innate, so it is not learning, but only remembering. This knowledge has been written in our minds and hearts; in fact, it is in every cell of our being. We are not, nor do we come into the world as "blank slates", though we do require proper nurturing, for we do have built in our spirit/mind/body archetypal structures that can unfold to the highest orders of creation.

Who is God's heir that they may be recognized? Where can the face of Christ be witnessed, so that the memory of God can return? Who can and must demonstrate true forgiveness, so that the restoration of the original condition is recalled?

You and me; you are the Offspring of That which we conveniently call God. Witness the face of Christ in every creature. We can and must demonstrate true forgiveness. Be still and know that your True Self is It; that your Self expresses as the Logos, which is that blueprint of which we are an analogue (another Logos) to the Creator. Contemplate and think on these words from <u>A Course in Miracles</u>:

> [...] the face of Christ is the great symbol of forgiveness. It is salvation. It is the symbol of the real world. Whoever looks on this no longer sees the world. He is as near to Heaven as is possible outside the gate. Yet from this gate it is no more than just a step inside. It is the final step. And this we leave to God.
>
> Forgiveness is a symbol too, but as the symbol of His Will alone it cannot be divided. And so the unity that it reflects becomes His Will. It is the only thing still in the world in part, and yet the bridge to Heaven.
>
> God's will is all there is. We can but go from nothingness to everything; from hell to Heaven. [...]
>
> How lovely does the world become in just that

> single instant when you see the truth about yourself reflected there. Now you are sinless and behold your sinlessness. Now you are holy and perceive it so. And now the mind returns to its Creator; the joining of the Father and the Son, the Unity of unities that stands behind all joining but beyond them all. God is not seen but understood. His Son is not attacked but recognized.[40]

Let us look upon the face of Christ and be forgiven. Whose image and similitude are we created in anyway? It's that which we call God, YHWH (the Tetragrammaton); our True Self is the Christ of God. We have realized this, and we are continually actualizing this. Our function is to forgive until not one thought of unforgiveness remains. Our function is to see all of humanity as the holy Sons/Daughters/Siblings of a Father/Mother/Child God in expression. We are endowed with wholeness and holiness, and all the attributes of God His creations possess. This is a day of great rejoicing; this is the day minds are healed, the day true perception leads us to knowledge, the day conscious awareness of the Self returns. And as the multitudes awaken to and acknowledge their own Christ Consciousness, the Second Coming manifests collectively. Look for it.

Now do we join Jesus in becoming saviors unto the world, becoming what Jesus became - totally identified with the Christ. The light that lights every man that comes into the world: this is the Christ/Logos, which is our Ultimate Self.

It is our function, duty, and purpose to see the face of Christ in all our fellow human beings and even in the rest of the animal kingdom so as to remember God, just as Jesus did for he lead the way. This is experienced by being gentle; by being so the world will be transformed. It is His Will, yet it is our will as well, that we awaken to this one and only Shared Will, knowing that there is no other. There is no peace in separation; unity with all and everything is what peace is. We are worthy, blessed, holy, divine beings. The depth of our being knows that this is so. Know the Authority within you.

Study and meditate on the fact that <u>you</u> remain as God created you. Look to the Superconsciousness within yourself, thereby finding God and your Real Self. In so doing you embark upon your path of individuation, realizing and actualizing all of your potential - Your path, Your Christhood. Then you will know from the depths of your own Self-Realization that you too are the way, the truth, and the life. Therefore, we affirm - I am, that is the Christ within is, the way, the truth, and the life, with God expressing as me.

The Divine Birth

I would like to cite a quote from a very famous Christian mystic, Meister Eckhart (1260-1329) because his comments reflect someone who had the mystical, numinous experiences that testify to what this writing is written for:

> God gives birth to the Son as you, as me, as each one of us. As many beings – as many gods in God. In my soul, God not only gives birth to me as his son, he gives birth to me as himself, and himself as me.
>
> I find in this divine birth that God and I are the same: I am what I was and what I shall always remain, now and forever. I am transported above the highest angels; I neither decrease nor increase, for in this birth I have become the motionless cause of all that moves. I have won back what has always been mine. Here, in my own soul, the greatest of all miracles has taken place – God has returned to God![41]

Let us give birth today to the child of God, the son and the daughter of the One, which is our ultimate self that we too may know beyond any doubt of mere intellectuality that we are at one with the One. Let us breathe in the animating spirit of the cosmic mystery of life itself that we receive when we bring in a deep breath, and thereby recognize and accept our connection that is born of and with the heavenly order.

Chapter 2

Cosmic Consciousness

Before going into the scripture passages that support the thesis of this manuscript, I find it most useful to make two quotes from a book that was first released in 1901. The book is entitled <u>Cosmic Consciousness, A Study in the Evolution of the Human Mind</u>, written by Richard Maurice Bucke, M.D. These quotes are so astute and appropriate for the task at hand, they are two wonderful informational gems:

> What is Cosmic Consciousness? [...] Cosmic Consciousness, then, is a higher form of consciousness than that possessed by the ordinary man. [...]
>
> Cosmic Consciousness is a third form which is as far above Self Consciousness as is that above Simple Consciousness. With this form, of course, both simple and self consciousness persist (as simple consciousness persists when self consciousness is acquired), but added to them is the new faculty so often named and to be named in this volume. The prime characteristic of cosmic consciousness is, as its name implies, a consciousness of the cosmos, that is, of the life and order of the universe. [...] Along with the consciousness of the cosmos there occurs an intellectual enlightenment or illumination which alone would place the individual on a new plane of existence - would make him almost a member of a new species. To this is added a state of moral exaltation, an indescribable feeling of elevation, elation, and joyousness, and a quickening of the moral sense, which is fully as striking and more important both to the individual and to the race than is the enhanced intellectual power. With these come, what may be called a sense of immortality, a consciousness of eternal life, not a conviction that he shall have this, but the consciousness that he has it already.
>
> Only a personal experience of it, or a prolonged study of men who have passed into the new life, will enable us to realize what this actually is; [...]
>
> The Saviour of man is Cosmic Consciousness - in

Paul's language - the Christ. The cosmic sense (in whatever mind it appears) crushes the serpent's head - destroys sin, shame, the sense of good and evil as contrasted one with the other, and will annihilate labor, though not human activity. [42]

Just think of it, as humanity evolves with more and more of us having numinous experiences we will realize that God is not just found at some church, which doesn't mean one shouldn't be apart of a gregarious community; as we have these numinous experiences it will be as a revelation to that individual, and as a result one will see that God is not confined to any particular sacred book or that only some licensed minister has the Word. People will have the direct knowing of their Source and it will be a wonderful thing. As we evolve the whole need to be takers or to be grasping at things will subside because as this faculty of Cosmic Consciousness grows and develops one will freely give of themselves knowing that there is more to give. People that obtain this will surely demonstrate exceptional capacities, radiant health, attractive dispositions and someone you'd find appealing to be around. Back to Dr. Bucke:

The faculty itself has many names, but they have not been understood or recognized. It will be well to give some of them here. They will be better understood as we advance. Either Gautama himself, or some one of his early disciples, called it "Nirvana" because of the "extinction" of certain lower mental faculties (such as the sense of sin, fear of death, desire of wealth, etc, etc.) which is directly incident upon its birth. This subjugation of the old personality along with the birth of the new is, in fact, almost equivalent to the annihilation of the old and the creation of the new self. The word Nirvana is defined as "the state to which the Buddhist saint is to aspire as the highest aim and highest good." Jesus called the new condition "the Kingdom of God" or the "Kingdom of Heaven," because of the peace and happiness which belong to it and which are perhaps its most characteristic features. Paul called it "Christ." He speaks of himself as "a man in Christ," of "them that are in Christ." He also calls it "the Spirit" and "the Spirit of God." After Paul had entered Cosmic consciousness he knew Jesus had possessed the cosmic sense and that he was living (as it were) the life of Jesus - that another individuality, another self, lived in him. This second self he called Christ (the divinely sent deliverer), identifying it not so much with the man Jesus, as with the deliverer which was to be sent and which had been sent in his person, who was both Jesus (the ordinary self conscious man) and Messiah (the herald and exemplar of the new, higher race). [...] Mohammed called the cosmic sense "Gabriel'" and seems to have looked upon it as a distinctly separate person who lived in him and spoke to him. Dante called it "Beatrice" ("Making Happy"), a name almost or equivalent to "Kingdom of Heaven." Balzac called the new man a "specialist" and the new condition "Specialism." Whitman called cosmic consciousness "My Soul," but spoke of it as if it were another person;[43]

A major point of this quote is to drive home the fact that this Christ Conscious faculty is an inherent power, ability, and a possessed capacity we have by being human (having a human mind), though we have to cultivate it, though admittedly some have to work harder at it than others. Accepting the facts of our creation certainly helps activate this faculty. Therefore, I pray that my effort in writing this material assists not only me but others in this process of going from self consciousness to cosmic consciousness. Again, this extended quote should lay the final groundwork before going directly into the Bible passages.

It's In The Holy Bible

What I have attempted to do in citing the work of Dr. Jung, Dr. Bucke, Dr. Errico, and Manly P. Hall is to present a case that not only supports, but gives certain evidence of a Collective Christ Consciousness, with humanity in possession of It and/or of It being available to humanity. However, due to our place in time and space (history), the culture that we live in, the conditioning that has resulted from programming – parental, societal, and religious indoctrination, citing these works alone is not enough. Due to such a heavy insistence upon the Bible as truth, I will cite passages from the Holy Bible, though from various renditions, which should go a long way to provide evidence that the Christ is not just confined to Jesus, that there is also the Collective Self or a Collective Christ, with the rest of humanity being at-one with God, possessing divinity and wholeness.

Truth

While the Bible does contain truth, truth didn't stop becoming manifest to humanity when the books of the Bible were compiled. The truth is ever-present; the truth is not confined to only one resource, and to believe so is idolatry. The fact is, the Truth embodies itself through a multitude of channels, while the Source remains One. Furthermore, to hold the belief that only the Bible is the source of truth or that only the Bible is inspired by God, and that since its compiling all inspiration has stopped or is less important is to place limitations on That which has none, and is to deny the very motivation of your own being. To hold this belief is a fixation in consciousness, yet Life goes on despite all fixations. So to those who are held by this belief system, know that YOU are, your Self is more than your previous conditioning; your release awaits you. Examine with me the evidence.

Only Jesus?

Beginning with some of the teachings of conventional Christianity - that only Jesus was and is capable of performing miracles, that only Jesus is the Son of God, and that only Jesus is divine, that only Jesus was and is sinless - this teaching is erroneous. It must be known that the Master Himself taught otherwise. For it is my proclamation that what Jesus claimed for him, he claimed for all of humanity by calling us to our divinity. Therefore we, as the rest of humanity, can be conduits of "miracles", with the Holy Spirit being the mechanism if we would but invoke and develop our talents. All of humanity expresses as the One Body of Christ, the Only Son of God. And yes, while we are truly human, we are not merely so, for we are definitely divine beings. Let's look at Jesus' own words.

In Jesus' Words

Now, in support of the words that I write are truth, I will cite Jesus' own words. From the Catholic Study Bible, let's begin with John 14:12: "Amen, amen, I say to you, whoever believes in me will do the works that I do, and will do greater ones than these, because I am going to the Father." What a great power we have within us, the very Kingdom of Heaven. Jesus would never have said this if the capacity to perform these works were not inherently available within us. We have been invited to perform miracles, so as to extend the Kingdom of God; in truth they are natural, corrective, healing, and universal. Another quote, from Matt 5:48, "So be perfect, just as your Heavenly Father is perfect." Would Jesus have made the statement to us if the potential were not inherently available to be actualized? In this writing I am pleased to leave the definition of perfect at being whole and complete as we are, because here is the culture hero, the "savior", the Master of Masters saying you can obtain perfection and being greater than him. Therefore, it's time for all this other kind of contrary teachings in his name to cease.

His prayer in Matt. 6:9 was to "Our Father". His prayer wasn't to MY Father, as if he had some sort of exclusiveness that the rest of humankind doesn't share. To him we are brothers and sisters of equality.

Yet another quote from Matt 10: 40, "Whoever receives

you receives me, and whoever receives me receives the one who sent me." This passage makes it ever so clear that in welcoming you, I welcome God. For as Paul writes in 1 Cor. 15:28, "When everything is subjected to him, then the Son himself will [also] be subjected to the one who subjected everything to him, so that God is all in all." You and I being part of creation means that **we are in the All, that we are an aspect of the All, and that every cell of our being is an expression of IT, because we cannot be outside of the All.** Ask yourself, can you be outside of the All? No way, so don't think other ways. This implies that Natural phenomena are expressions of God, i.e. you. Truly consider and know that which we call God IS the ALL in ALL, our purpose here is to awaken to this reality and thus live accordingly. Now surely when I welcome you, I do not welcome the person of Jesus, but I do, in fact, welcome the Christ of God. In receiving or welcoming God as You, the idea here is to look beyond the appearances and perceive both the holiness of the person and the divine image; this would be viewing things just as Genesis 1:27 states, "God created man in his image; in the divine image he created him; male and female he created them." Remember, too, that in the previous verse, 26, God said, "Let us make man in our image, after our likeness. Let them have dominion…" For it is in this way, looking out onto others from our own perception of holiness and divinity, and onto the holiness and divinity of others, that true practice of the Golden Rule can be displayed or exemplified in action.

An Idiom: "Believe in his name"

The scripture passage, John 14:12, brings to mind the phrase "believing in his name" or "praying in the name of Jesus". A very useful book entitled, <u>Let There Be Light: The Seven Keys</u>, written by Dr. Rocco Errico, shines some light on the meaning of the idiomatic phrase "believing in his name":

> Semitic idiomatic phrases fill the Bible. Idioms in any language have at one time or another created misunderstandings. Biblical languages are no exception, for there are many idiomatic sayings in Scripture that are not easy to comprehend simply because they are translated literally.
>
> [...] The Aramaic phrase 'believe in his name' signifies 'believe in his teaching'.[44]

What a difference one word makes. To get clear on what the word "name" means in that phrase from scripture makes a world of difference; it means comprehending various keys or threads that are interwoven together into a culture such as language, idioms of a language, the culture itself, psychology, symbolism, mysticism, and amplification that weaves an amazing mosaic, with certain word usages conveyed in an idiom for instance. That the idiomatic phrasing really means to believe in or accept the "teachings" of someone and not necessarily their "name" per se, provides one the ability to see beyond the surface teachings and into the bedrock of deeper understanding.

The Only-Begotten?

The bible, the various ones that can be found, use another phrase that makes Jesus appear to be so unlike the rest of us – "the only begotten of the Father", which is found in John 1:14. I will again quote Dr. Errico from his book, <u>Let There Be Light: The Seven Keys</u>, since he has spent years studying the Aramaic language:

> What did the writer of John's gospel mean by the expression 'only begotten'? Biblical authors often express spiritual ideas and truths in figurative speech and human terms. Therefore we can easily misunderstand the writer's meaning and intention. [...]
>
> In Aramaic *yeheedaya*, does not mean 'only begotten.' It means 'sole', 'only', 'precious', 'beloved', and 'one of a

kind'. The word also, by implication, refers to the 'firstborn son'.

People who speak Aramaic understand this expression literally when referring to their children, especially when distinguishing between the firstborn son and his father. But when they refer to God in this expression, they understand it figuratively. We must also discern the Eastern custom that is behind the meaning *yeheedaya*. [...]

In the Near East, the firstborn son is the *yeheedaya*, 'the sole heir' of all the father possesses. This 'beloved son' is the glory and honor of his father. He is the one who will succeed his father, carry his name, and inherit his business. He will also be in charge of all his father's household [...].

John uses this term *yeheedaya* to mean that Jesus expressed a unique and beloved relationship with God as a father. Jesus' life was a vital and powerful manifestation of divine sonship. Therefore, he became known as the 'sole heir' and 'uniquely beloved son' of this universal and spiritual truth of divine sonship for the human family.

In his letter to the Romans, Paul says that Jesus is 'the firstborn among many brethren.' According to the New Testament, we come to understand that we and all nationalities are children of God through the teachings of the Messiah.

An Eastern father glories when he sees his 'firstborn son', because he sees himself re-created in his offspring. This is what John is saying about God as a father: 'the glory as of the only son of the Father'.[45]

How often does humanity make anthropocentric analogies to attempt to explain various types of relationships, and the relationship humanity has with God is right up there in the anthropomorphizing. How great to get an understanding of the scriptures within the context of the keys as Dr. Errico places them, and not just from some super-imposition that has placed the historical Jesus upon some pedestal that the rest of humanity cannot attain. How refreshing to realize this term *yeheedaya* was the same term used by those who spoke Aramaic when referring to their own children, and for possibly the lack of another term it was used figuratively when referring to God. Think about this word *yeheedaya,* meaning *firstborn,* and not this nebulous, shrouded, English 'only begotten' idea. It's just one more attempt by those who would want to subjugate you, to make you think you are less than Jesus even in potential; we are not less than him, and St. Paul helps clarify the situation. Therefore, and remembering the teachings of the Logos that *we are one,* it is understood that it's the Christ that is the only Son of the Heavenly Father, with Jesus being the firstborn of many brethren and us as co-heirs within the Christ Sonship.

We Are One

Now here are a few other quotes from Jesus teaching of our oneness or unity, which is what the Logos should and does instruct: "On that day you will realize that I am in my Father and you in me, and I in you."[46] And here is another one from John 17:20-24:

> "I pray not only for them, but also for those who will believe in me through their word, so that they may all be one, as you, Father, are in me and I in you, that they also may be in us, that the world may believe that you sent me. And I have given then the glory you gave me, so that they may be one, as we are one, I in them and you in me, that they may be brought to perfection as one, that the world may know that you sent me, and that you loved them even as you loved me. Father, they are your gift to me, I wish that where I am they also may be with me, that they may see my glory that you gave me, because you loved me before the foundation of the world."[47]

This passage alone should cease all so-called teachings from any minister of the day that says we are separate from God, period. Any person that goes around teaching something contrary to us being One is not teaching "in his name", i.e., what Jesus as the Logos taught. His teaching is that we are One, therefore, any so-called Christian and all the more so a ministerial "authority" type, who tries to make the rest of humanity out to be *less than one*, that we are somehow separate from God and from Jesus in reality is simply wrong, and as a result that person would not be "believing in his teaching". Any idea that someone may have that is contrary to these needs to be worked through and re-thought so as to get the understanding/knowing/feeling that your real Self is at-one with Jesus/God. This statement by Jesus was not just meant for his apostles, it includes you and me even now. For in the New Scofield Reference Bible, the Authorized King James Version, in the commentary notes to this passage, one can read that the word "those" in verse 20 refers to "all Christians throughout the whole age," while the word "their" in the same verse implicates his apostles.[48]

These two passages sum up what creation is in its totality and reality - **One**. With these two passages spoken by Christ through Jesus, He summed up the Communicative Property of Equality that A=B, B=C, A=C. God is Christ (as Jesus), Christ Jesus is divinely human (exemplifies humanity), and God is (expresses as) Humanity. Time and again one can hear certain views about taking the Bible literal, so here is Jesus saying "I and the Father are one and you are one with me," therefore, you can't but conclude this Communicative Property of Equality. Humankind is the expression of God on earth. Yes, in one way God is more, but He is never less than His creations, and for sure we are an aspect of the Greater Godhead, yet always in containment of the Whole. So like Jesus before us we can truly claim that I AM. For we are At-one with the One, the Creator and His/Her creations are inseparable. Here again is the quote from Luke 17: 20-21:

> When some of the Pharisees asked Jesus when the kingdom of God would come, he answered, saying to them, The Kingdom of God does not come by observation. Neither will they say, Behold, it is here, or behold, it is there! For, behold, the kingdom of God is within you.[49]

By Jesus' own account "The Kingdom of God **Is Within You.** I don't have to make any of this up, these comments are right there to <u>behold</u>. Jesus is also quoted as saying, "Reform your lives! **The Kingdom of Heaven is at hand"** (Matt 4:17). It is the same theme that John the Baptist asserts by, "Reform your lives! The reign of God is at hand" (Matt 3:2). If these two figures are using such words to convey **where** and **when** the kingdom is, then it is high time we start acting upon it **within** ourselves and right **now**, not in some future life after we die from this plane of existence. Things that are at hand are visible, though not necessarily in some empiricist/logical positivist way. We have to see not with our senses per se, but rather see with our mind's eye or with cognition.

The Blessed Trinity

The fact that we are One with the I AM Presence brings up a couple more issues to be dealt with, and then I will return to the words of Jesus. First, if one wants to view God as Triune, a Trinity, just where does humanity fit in? In earlier religious training I was taught that God as the Father was the first aspect of the Trinity, that Jesus was the second aspect, referred to as the Son, and that the Holy Spirit was the third and the Communication aspect between the first two; though the rest of humanity was somehow separate and apart from this Blessed Trinity.

How can this be, if we are to take Jesus' own words from John 17:20 that, "I am in my Father, and you in me and I in you"? It is simply this: The second aspect of the Trinity, the Son, is all of Humanity. It is just that we, collectively, must awaken to it. Let's be clear on this - there is only One Son of God - it is the Christ/Logos, "the light that gives light to **EVERY** man that comes into the world." Understand that Christ is unified spirit expressing itself infinitely throughout creation; to teach that only Jesus is part of the Trinity is not the absolute truth. Jesus himself taught otherwise and so does

Paul in his epistles. Humanity is collectively the Body of Christ, which makes us part of the Trinity.

Let us look at what Paramahansa Yogananda writes about the threefold nature of God as Father, Son, and Holy Spirit in his book, <u>Autobiography of a YOGI</u>:

> God the Father is the Absolute, Unmanifested, existing **beyond** vibratory creation. God the Son is the Christ Consciousness existing **within** vibratory creation; this Christ Consciousness is the "only begotten" or sole reflection of the Uncreated Infinite. The outward manifestation of the omnipresent Christ Consciousness, it's "witness" (Revelation 3:14), is **Aum**, the Word or Holy Ghost: invisible divine power, the only doer, the sole causative and activating force that upholds all creation through vibration. **Aum** the blissful Comforter is heard in meditation and reveals to the devotee the ultimate Truth, bringing "all things to... remembrance."[50]

God as a Quaternion

It is good to also point out that God can be viewed as a set of four instead of just three. From a Catholic Church view point it takes the form of the Assumption of Mary, not just her soul but with her body, into heaven. This is an ultimate recognition of her as a goddess and turns or evolves the Trinity into a Quaternary. The beauty of this is that, for the Church, it finally acknowledges the feminine aspect of creation, and that is a good thing. Elaborating on this though is really beyond the scope of this writing, yet one can get their fill of this idea in Jung's Volume 11 of the collected works, <u>Psychology and Religion: West and East</u>, 2nd Edition.[51]

Original Blessing & Holiness

Another topic to deal with is this: since we are One, then we must be like Jesus in every way, not only in being divine, but also as being sinless. Jesus did not say "you are like me in every way except sin", this is merely man's teaching; Jesus' teaching is explicit - "You and I are one." Note what the Gospel of John 9:16 says: "So some of the Pharisees said, 'This man is not from God, because he does not keep the sabbath.' [But] others said, 'How can a sinful man do such signs?"[52]

Some of the authorities of the day thought Jesus was not from God, i.e. sinful, therefore, we have to consider ourselves in the same light as Jesus. So this concept that we are "original sinners" or that we have this original sin just embedded in us somewhere comes across as nothing but another attempt to mentally and physically control humanity. This is not implying that we are mistake-free; it just may not be some offence against God as theology would have it. It means that when we do "miss the mark", which is what sin means, we do but a retake, as if we were making a movie. To teach that humans are marred from the beginning as sinners and that we can never escape sin is to mock God. It is this logical: since we were created by God, then we as His/Her creations must be, in some fashion, like God (holy and divine), and must contain an original blessing. If God is holy, then I am holy because He/She could only create like Him/Herself. My Self-Image is that of God: we are holy, whole, pure, and complete. Being a Christian means taking on Jesus' teachings, not someone else's controlling ideas about his teachings. Jesus' teachings are to 'be perfect', so I am taking His word for it. Or when he healed someone saying 'go and sin no more', meaning when we put on the new self we can finally escape sin. Remember, what is the teaching of the Logos? That we are one, as from the Gospel of John, "I and the Father are one and you are one with me". Therefore, our function is to increase our *proportion* at being and expressing godliness.

Whichever way we perceive ourselves to be, holy or sinful, we will act in accordance with this image because fidelity to premises is a law of mind. Therefore, we have to ask ourselves, 'Is this action holy or sinful (missing the mark)'? Premises and/or perceptions are acted out behaviorally. This is self-fulfilling prophecy. Since "all things came into being through Him and apart from Him nothing came to be," then we take on the attitude that, "No one who is begotten of God commits sin, because God remains in him; he cannot sin because he is begotten of God."[53]   This quote, which is right there in the Bible, is not just talking about Jesus, it includes us.   Therefore, let us then contemplate some of Paul's words, "We know that our old self was crucified with him so that the body of sin might be destroyed , and we might no longer be enslaved to sin….So you also must consider yourselves dead to sin and alive to God in Christ Jesus."[54] Remember it is this ultimate Self of ours that is Christed, which "cannot sin", therefore, live in the Christed Self, which is beyond just the ego or the shadow.

Viewing Sin Psychologically

It is important to view sin and a few other related religious ideas psychologically, from a Depth Psychological perspective and not just view it dogmatically because by doing so we can get an understanding about the intrapsychic problems that those Church authorities had who originated such teachings who have projected from their own psyche a particular Self image onto their idea of what is the divine. Very briefly the Church doctrine is that humanity (in perpetuity) has this original sin because they have viewed all of us as identified with Adam who disobeyed, rejected or rebelled against God and therefore we are fallen, whereas Jesus Christ is identified with God, subsequently our relationship with God has to be reconnected or bought by Jesus' suffering. Suffering is not necessarily the wages of sin, but rather from a creation centered model of spirituality suffering is the birth pangs of the universe. Lionel Corbett, Professor of Depth Psychology writes thus:

> […] This particular line of development of the original

story is so forced when viewed against the actual life of Jesus that it must be understood in terms of the personal psychopathology of its originators and of those who accepted it. For example, according to Augustine, the necessary transmission of sin occurs by virtue of sexuality, which is inherently sinful. This is an understandable projection in view of the difficulty Augustine is known to have had with sexuality, so it is no surprise that he would seize on Paul's writing in this way. We may infer that 'Paul' (at least the writer to whom Paul's name is attributed) had some similar difficulty, a common affliction among intensely patriarchal men with mother problems. Modern theologians have sought to modify the notion of original sin by suggesting that it simply represents our human heritage, which makes us heir to sin because we are all bound by prevailing cultural problems. But this only transfers the reason for our 'badness' to some other, inevitable and external, cause. It perpetuates the projection of the complex onto society instead of dealing with those aspects of it that represent an intrapsychic problem. [55]

Therefore, rather than referring to sin as "the breaking of official rules" regarding ones behaviors, sin is to be defined and comprehended psychologically as behavior which,

> [...] arises out of intrapsychic splits which represent infantile selfobject needs. In such a case, the Self reveals itself in psychopathology. A psychological understanding of redemption follows from this argument, namely the healing of such splits within ourselves. Jung (CW 18, 1687) notes that the archetype of the Redeemer is present in all of us, which is why the story of a Messiah is so important. Christianity insists that redemption is only possible by means of belief in Christ, but practical psychotherapeutic experience suggests that the archetype of redemption may manifest in other ways. [56]

The idea of the archetype of redemption manifesting in other ways is taken up very thoroughly by Joseph Campbell in his book aptly titled, The Hero With A Thousand Faces.[57]

A New Perceptual Order - A New Penitential Rite

Now to firm up this perceptual shift away from *sinful humanity* and onto the fact of our God-Image, so as to call it forth. That is, in an attempt to heal any intrapsychic splits within ourselves let us realize that it is the psyche that is the sacramental container, which results in making spirituality and psychology synonymous. What is religious varies very extensively; therefore, the viewpoint to this is focusing in on whatever is numinous for the individual because the Self can manifest in a myriad of fashions. [58]

The idea in changing our perceptual view away from sin is to leave behind the guilt that is inherent in the concept and jargon of "sinning against God". Take the view that guilt possesses a type of automatic feedback system that can perpetuate the error. When I think of this phrase of "sinning against God", it seems useful to me, in an effort to stop doing this would be to begin using some different terminology. A suitable substitute word is *misapplied decision*. Its inherent implication is that it will make people more conscious of what is happening in their lives, and give them a realization of choice, with the idea to choose again to heal any split within oneself. Subsequently they won't react on some conditioned, spinal level or mid-brain-emotional level, but respond from a higher rational, cortical matter and displaying those characteristics that speak of an internal locus of control. They will be living from their own Inner Guidance and not on someone else's belief system, and people will get on with the process of individuation. Harmony and peace will prevail because others will be viewed as extensions of ourselves; yes, the golden rule will be the order of the day because we will all be seeing the other as ourselves.

Since the psyche is the sacramental container and what is numinous varies among individuals, one thing to bring out, due to its personal meaning and impact it has had on me; and one way I see this perceptual shift occurring globally is for the structure of the Order of Mass in Catholicism to be rewritten and revised. Beginning with the Penitential Rite the service focuses on the error, or the "separation", which is the meaning of the "fall". This is where the whole concept of sin entered, that is, with the identification of being solely a body. But even while in a body we are at-one with Spirit, never in reality separate. It is to this renewed awareness that is being called forth, so as to know with certainty that just because we are embodied doesn't make us guilty of anything, rather we are alive in the creative energy of God, whole and complete. We have been redeemed. Know that our Heavenly Father and Earthly Mother are pleased with us Sons and Daughters, for we remain as God created us, which is "good". For those not familiar with the Penitential Rite, which appears in every Monthly or Seasonal Missalette, it follows thus:

> I confess to almighty God,
> and to you, my brothers and sisters,
> that I have sinned through my own fault
> [We strike our breast]
> in my thoughts and in my words, in what I have done,
> and in what I have failed to do;
>   and I ask blessed Mary, ever virgin,
> all the angels and saints,
> and you, my brothers and sisters,
> to pray for me to the Lord our God.
> May almighty God have mercy on us,
>   forgive us our sins,
>   and bring us to everlasting life.
> Amen.

Surely this penitence does not offer a vision of transcendence, therefore, I offer a New Penitential Rite:

> I relate to Almighty God,
> And to you my brothers and sisters,

That I recognize that while I have made a mistake,
Through my own error, by way of thoughts and words,
By what has been done, and what has failed to be done,
Yet it was not a sinful evil to be punished; no it was
Rather a missing of the mark that needs to be but corrected
Or even an intrapsychic split within myself
That needs to be but healed,
So that its negative and undesirable consequences may cease
That I may again live within the bounds of God's Law.
It was a lack of love, and so through acts of forgiveness
And of love do I make amends.
In doing so I accept the At-one-ment,
And am united with my Loving and Supportive Creator,
And also with you my brothers and sisters.
God, You not only have had mercy on us,
You have told us that no one begotten of You can sin.
This is more than the historical Jesus,
This is the Christ of Faith, which is in us.
And makes humanity part of the Trinity.
So we thank You for bringing us to the awareness of
Our indispensability within the Eternal Kingdom.
My error is undone now, for I have chosen again,
And I am gently awakened to
The consciousness of my redemption and reconciliation.
I go forth now looking upon my sinlessness
Along with my brothers and sisters in Christ
Acting in accordance with the Laws of Life,
And communing with the Heavenly Father
And Earthly Mother and their Angelic Forces
Which is the Tree of Life. Amen.

We Are Worthy

Another change that will go a long way toward
redirecting our energy is the statement in the Liturgy of the
Eucharist, "Lord I am not worthy to receive you, but only say
the word and I shall be healed." This "not worthy" attitude
places one in a perception of valuelessness. And furthermore,

it makes a church service (mass) no celebration, but rather an outright mind control suggestive technique over God's children. The Word has indeed already been given, and God's word is essentially that the one, the individual, has a worth beyond price in the Kingdom of Heaven, that God is "ever mindful" of man. The parable of the Good Shepherd and the prodigal son also supports the value of the one. So I thank You Lord for counting us worthy to receive You, for You have said the Word and I am healed. You are even saying the word now, thereby keeping me whole. Matt. 11:11 shows exactly the worth in which Jesus views us: "Truly I tell you, among those born of women no one has arisen greater than John the Baptist; yet the least in the kingdom of heaven is greater than he."[59] Jesus also says in Matt. 12:11-12: "Suppose one of you has only one sheep and it falls into a pit on the sabbath; will you not lay hold of it and lift it out? How much more valuable is a human being than a sheep."[60]

It's time to accept and embrace the verdict that the very man or rather God as Jesus, the "savior" to millions worldwide, casts upon humanity – we are precious. Just because we are embodied does not make us, automatically, wretched or original sinners, or anything negative for that matter. We are very worthy of receiving all the gifts that our loving Creator has to give, and so we accept. In so doing we attune our minds and our hearts to what the gifts of the Kingdom are and set the process in motion for them to come to us in abundance and in certainty.

More of Jesus' Words

Now here are more scripture passages:

"Is it not written in your law, 'I have said, 'You are gods'? If it calls them gods to whom the word of God came, and scripture cannot be set aside, can you say that the one whom the Father has consecrated and sent into the world blasphemes because I said, 'I am the Son of God'?"[61]

Jesus reiterating the words from Psalms 82:6 says: "You are gods, children of the Most High, all of you." Jesus is calling us gods. Can we be with the fact that, "We are gods!! Do we even know how to relate to this idea and fact? Whose image and similitude are we created in anyway? Many people as of yet cannot, that is why Psalm 82:7 reads, "nevertheless, you shall die like mortals, and fall like any prince."[62] We die like men we because don't entertain and develop our Godly powers, so many stay in the muck and mire of being merely human. Like it or not we, as humanity, are creators, and we are creating heavenly realities or hellish ones right now here on earth. So what are we choosing? Everything that Jesus claimed and worked for we can, we must, we will, and every good thing attributed to Jesus by the Church we share in, for it is our purpose here on earth to become as Him. These words that I write are only those which the Father has told me; For it is not I but He who does the work through me, just as Jesus said the same of/toward himself. We are co-creators with God; therefore we are imbued with the same loving will to create.

> "You are indeed the light of the world... Let your light so shine before men that they may see your good works and glorify your Father in heaven. "[63]

Jesus is saying that **You** provide knowledge and show others the way while you are in the world. And he says to let this light of **ours** shine so that men will see goodness in our acts. I am thankful that salvation comes from grace and not from any act of ours lest we boast, yet Jesus sure is making the point that "Faith without works is dead." Paradoxical, yes. While we are in the world our function is to be bearers of truth. And remember its "Our" Father with whom we are "At-One" with. Here is another quote of Jesus':

"Truly, truly, I say to you, he who believes in me shall do
the works which I do, and even greater than these things
he shall do, because I am going to my Father."[64]

What a great power we have within us, the very
Kingdom of Heaven. Jesus would have never said this if the
capacity to perform these works were not inherently present
within us. We have been invited to perform miracles, so as to
extend the Kingdom of God. In truth they are natural,
corrective, healing, and universal.

We have been given the Spirit of the strength of God
and truth, not of doubt and fear. So we are capable of
performing the miracles that our Guidance tells us to. By our
spoken words and deeds will the "miracles" be performed,
and only by doing them will we release ourselves from
limitation and experience freedom. Jesus identified himself as
the "least" one, as the greatest one, and even as ourself - this is
the totality of the universal Christ, the Christ who takes form
in all of humanity and not in just one manifestation. After all,
God is the "all in all." Realize what the **ALL-IN-ALL** means
and awaken to it; and also consider what the author of The
Acts says, "For in him we live, and move, and have our being
in God; as certain also of your own poets have said, For we are
also his off spring."[65]

Consider that every cell that composes our body lives,
moves, and has its being in water. All research reveals the fact
that the phenomenon called "Life" (organic life) only manifests
in water. From a scientific point of view water is the vehicle
of life. From a spiritual point of view God is Life. Therefore
we must conclude that every cell, tissue, organ and system of
our body, being part of all that there is, can forth-rightfully be
labeled "God". So can this book, the writer and the reader, for
we are in no way outside of the All. Can you be outside of
the All? No. The situation could be described as *panentheistic,*
which is that *all things are in God and God is in all things*; there is
no duality in panentheism, unlike theism which teaches that

God is just "out there" with God and His creations separate.

The passages up to now have been supportive of our unity and complete connection with God and our inherent sameness with Jesus. Also the passages have given us a clue as to our worth beyond price within the Kingdom. For in the end all must and will be saved, and return to God. There must not be one "soul" eternally damned; to have even one eternally damned would render the Kingdom incomplete. The only thing that will be "eternally punished" will be those characteristics, but not that which has been created, for if the created is damned, God is damned. The purpose of the Son is not to condemn the world, but to save it. The unconditional love of the Good Shepherd will go after the "lost sheep" until they are convinced. God created all; to condemn any part of creation would be to condemn Himself, and that is not going to happen. It is the same thing in physics: no matter has ever been totally destroyed; matter is simply rearranged and shifted to another place.

The Christ: A Psychological Image of Wholeness

The next Scripture passages will be ones that support the psychological position of the Christ symbol, where Jesus relays some parables:

> The kingdom of heaven may be likened to a man who sowed good seed in his field.
>
> The kingdom of heaven is like a mustard seed that a person took and sowed in a field. It is the smallest of all seeds, yet when full-grown it is the largest of plants.
>
> The kingdom of heaven is like a treasure buried in a field, which a person finds and hides again, and out of joy goes and sells all that he has and buys that field. [66]

The "field" in these three passages refers to one's

psyche: conscious and unconscious.   Again, to repeat, this takes us to the reality that it is the psyche that is sacramental, that the sacramental container is the psyche.   The mustard seed and the treasure represent thoughts in consciousness. Perception of Heaven has been achieved; Contact made.   For Heaven or hell is but a state of consciousness, and so is the perception of The Christ.   These are the *consciousness as the ground of all being* comprehension of Jesus' teachings; the truth is that the Kingdom is - Consciousness.   If one is going to be in Heaven, being Aware that one is there is certainly in order. And if one is Aware of something, then that means that one is Conscious of that thing.   It (the Kingdom) is not per se some geographical location; rather it is our relation with God. Again from the science of physics, we know that matter and energy are interchangeable, that matter is not solid per se but actually exists in "fields of energy."   This can mean that the atoms and molecules of our cells, the tissues and organs of our bodies vibrate at certain frequencies (resonance) and coalesce into what we are.   It can also mean that those thoughts which dominate a human's psyche will act like electro-magnets and attract into that person's "field" or life space whatever is being thought about.   Let's consider another passage:

> Again, the kingdom of heaven is like a merchant's search
> for fine pearls. When he finds   a pearl of great price, he
> goes and sells all that he has and buys it.[67]

The valuable pearl is like the mustard seed and the treasure - a thought in consciousness, with the merchant becoming aware that it reflects heaven.

One last passage that I will cite in accordance with the Christ figure being a psychological image of wholeness is the passage of Jesus speaking with the Samaritan woman in John 4:14: "...But whoever drinks the water I shall give him will never thirst; the water I shall give will become in him a spring of water welling up to eternal life."[68] This verse is clearly an example that indicates that the "waters" are in reference to the mind, with the mind being the gateway to the reservoir of infinity, the spirit. We really have to be with the truth as to where Jesus says the fountain is: **WITHIN**. It's within us. Then we are to look out onto the world from this kingdom within view. We have to simply be with this. Talk with many of these so-called "fundamentalist Christians" and bring up the fact that the Power is within us and not from some external church or from God who is in a far off remote heaven, and see what they say; I am praying that the ones I spoke with were neophytes and just didn't know any better. I have been citing passages from the Bible, not just something I am making up, therefore, contemplate and meditate on these facts.

"*Christ exemplifies the archetype of the self.*"[69] Christ is our very Self. Indeed as John 1 has it, it is Christ the Power "through whom all things came into being, and apart from him nothing came to be...The real light which gives light to every man...and who did accept him he empowered to become children of God." Christ is the power; Jesus is the pattern. Christ is the true image of God; our inner man is made in this likeness. Invisible, yet it manifests; incorporeal, yet it becomes flesh; incorrupt, indeed without sin; and immortal, truly having eternal life. In accordance with the **Principle of Correspondence**: As above, so below; as below, so above - the psychological image of above extends itself to the physical realms of below, thereby including all of the created universe as the expression of that which we call God. As above, so below is what the Star of David or Seal of Solomon symbolizes. Now note this example:

> John said to him, 'Teacher, we saw someone driving out demons in your name, and we tried to prevent him because he does not follow us.' Jesus replied, 'Do not prevent him. There is no one who performs a mighty deed in my name who can at the same time speak ill of me. Anyone who gives you a cup of water to drink because you belong to Christ, amen, I say to you, will

surely not lose his reward.'[70]

Jesus uses the word <u>Christ</u>, "you belong to Christ". He couldn't and would not have used the word Jesus, and so he did not. And how perfectly does John's comment describe that which divides the sects of Christianity. Let us grow in understanding and thereby come together in unity.

Christ is the power; Jesus is the pattern

Let us now consider a Catholic priest named Edward Schillebeeckx who wrote two books to clarify this very distinction: one entitled <u>Jesus: An Experiment in Christology</u>, the other <u>Christ: The Experience of Jesus as Lord</u>. The titles of these works practically say it all; consider the use of the word Christology, a study in what is the Christ; and think about how often the phrase *Jesus is Lord* can be heard or said, but here this title reads, *Jesus as Lord*. These titles, in a very sublime manner, tell one who is astute that Christ is the power and that Jesus is the pattern. The phrase *Jesus as Lord* says loud and clear that *the Lord* is something that is beyond or more than Jesus. A quote from Schillebeechx's *Foreword* to the <u>JESUS</u> book should give us a clue that even theologians realize this differentiation because he writes:

> This book is part of a more extensive Christological study. The second book examines in particular Pauline and Johannine doctrine, concentrating on the various Christologies of the New Testament itself. The first book, therefore, is a 'Jesus book', not altogether neglecting the Christ; whereas the second volume is a 'Christ book', with due reference to Jesus of Nazareth.[71]

The Office of the Christ

If the Christ is not confined to Jesus alone, then the function of the whole idea of what the Christ stands for has to be considered. Therefore, it is a good time to go over a definition regarding the *Office of the Christ*. In the book <u>The Book of Knowledge: The Keys of Enoch</u> the definition of this conception for us to behold is:

> The Redemptive Office of Divine Light, encompassing the work of the 144,000 Ascended Masters working with YHWH and Michael through Jesus the Christ for the purification of this fallen universe. This includes all of the Ascended Masters who work for the liberation of man throughout the world in all aeons of time.[72]

In the Hindu tradition Krishna would qualify as one of these Ascended Masters who works for the liberation of humanity and who occupied the Office of the Christ. Consider his name, which is in Sanskrit, though in Greek it means Christos, which is Christ.

From The Epistles of Paul

I turn now to the Epistles of Paul. He himself is very aware of the Christ Consciousness that is ever-present in all of humanity. His writings are more explicit on this topic than the gospels are because the gospels relay an experience in Christology, telling us of Jesus <u>as</u> Lord, while the Epistles tell us of "…the glory to be revealed in us. For the earnest expectation of all mankind waits for the manifestation of the sons of God", and "…the mystery of Christ in you, the hope of our glory."[73] In another epistle Paul writes:

> Now this I affirm and insist on in the Lord: you must no longer live as the Gentiles live, in the futility of their minds. They are darkened in their understanding, alienated from the life of God because of their ignorance and hardness of heart. They have lost all sensitivity and have abandoned themselves to licentiousness, greedy to practice every kind of impurity. **That is not the way you learned Christ! For surely you have heard about him and**

were taught in him, as truth is in Jesus. You were taught to put away your former way of life, your old self, corrupt and deluded by its lusts, and to be renewed in the spirit of your minds, and to **clothe yourselves with the new self**, created according to the likeness of God in true righteousness and holiness.[74] (Emphasis added).

Paul is very clear and totally certain that Christ is the power "which gives light to every man and who did accept Him He empowered to become children of God" and that Jesus is the model from which to draw from. What is that "...*new self, created according to the likeness of God...*"? It is The Christ, our True Self! The next passage to cite:

Let this mind be in you, which was also in Christ Jesus, Who, being in the form of God, thought it **not robbery to be equal with God**, but made himself of no reputation, and took upon Him the form of a servant, and was made in the likeness of men.[75] (Emphasis added).

Think what Paul is telling us, that it is basically okay and righteous that Jesus considered himself equal with God, and Paul is telling us to put on the mind that was in Christ Jesus; How bold it that? Not robbery to be equal with God! Go tell this one to a minister, for it's in the Bible! Here again, consider how a fundamentalist wants you to think, which is *literally*; okay, **if** you take what Paul is writing literally, **then** you have to conclude logically that if I put on the mind that was in Jesus, who by this time had attained Christhood, then when we get the thought that we are equal with God (because it's in the Bible) because we take it seriously and to heart Jesus' (the Logos) teaching *that we are one*, and one equals one, then it's NOT theft, we're not crooks, it's not a swindle, we're not pirates if we think we are equal with God. Contemporary Christians are so adamant about taking the Bible literally, so let's take this passage literally, and take it to heart.

So what is the ultimate point? It's to get the comprehension of what is God that we are in that image and similitude, which we can equate ourselves with, and that is that *we are creators*. God is to man as man is to his creations. Remember proportion, an even distribution of elements, an irreducible individual constituent of and for a whole; an essential entity contributing to a whole providing balance, harmony and symmetry. So just what is it that we are creating? Guess what, we are doing it all the time if we realize it or not. On a small scale we show that we are creators now, yet eventually we too will create on a grand, universal scale. So I have to give thanks to Master Jesus for affirming what our True Self is. Now to continue with Paul's writings:

> I do not want you to be unaware, brothers, that our ancestors were all under the cloud and all passed through the sea, and all of them were baptized into Moses in the cloud and in the sea. All ate the same spiritual food, and all drank the same spiritual drink, for they drank from a spiritual rock that followed them, and the rock was the Christ.[76]

Paul is recalling an account from the Old Testament at a point in time when Jesus was not yet born. Take note he doesn't call the rock *Jesus*, he calls the rock *Christ*, testifying to the Consciousness, to the Intelligible Logos blueprint pattern, and to the true origin of Power.

The whole chapter 8 of the book of Romans could be quoted but just most of it will be:

> There is, therefore, now no condemnation to them who are in Christ Jesus, who walk not after the flesh, but after the Spirit. For the law of the Spirit of life in Christ Jesus hath made me free from the law of sin and death. For what the law could not do, in that it was weak through the flesh, God sending his own Son, in the likeness of sinful flesh and for sin, condemned sin in the flesh. That the righteousness of the law might **be fulfilled in us,** who walk not after the flesh, but after the Spirit…
> But ye are not in the flesh but in the Spirit, if it so be that the Spirit of God dwell in you. Now if any man

have not the Spirit of Christ, he is none of his. And if Christ be in you, the body is dead because of sin, but the Spirit is life because of righteousness. But if the Spirit of him that raised up Jesus from the dead dwell in you, he that raised up Christ from the dead shall also give life to your mortal bodies by his Spirit that dwelleth in you...

For as many as are led by the Spirit of God, they are the sons of God. For ye have not received the spirit of bondage again to fear; but ye have received the spirit of adoption, whereby we cry, Abba, Father. The Spirit himself beareth witness with our spirit, that we are the children of God. And if children, then heirs - heirs to God, and **joint heirs with Christ** - if so be that we suffer with him, that we may be also glorified together.

For I reckon that the sufferings of this present time are not worthy to be compared with **the glory to be revealed** in us. For the earnest expectation of the creation waiteth for the manifestation of the sons of God. For the creation was made subject to vanity, not willingly but by reason of him who hath subjected the same in hope. Because **the creation itself also shall be delivered from the bondage of corruption** into the glorious liberty of the children of God. For we know that the whole creation groaneth and travaileth in pain together until now. And not only they, but **ourselves also, who have the first fruits of the Spirit,** even we ourselves groan within ourselves, waiting for the adoption, that is, the redemption of our body...

And he that searcheth the hearts knoweth what is the mind of the Spirit, because he maketh intercession for the saints according to the will of God.

And we know that all things work together for good to them that love God, to them who are the called according to his purpose. For whom he did foreknow, he also did predestinate to be conformed to the image of his Son, that he might be the firstborn among many brethren. Moreover, whom he did predestinate, them he also called; and whom he called, them he also justified, and whom he justified them he also glorified. What shall we then say to these things? If God *be* for us, who *can be* against us?

What shall separate us from the love of Christ?...For I am persuaded that neither death, nor life, nor angels, nor principalities, nor powers, **nor things** present, nor things to come, nor height, nor depth, nor any other creation, **shall be able to separate us from the love of God, which is in Christ Jesus, our Lord.**[77] (Emphasis and underline added).

That a good quote? Notice all the essential elements that go into putting on the mind of Christ, it is not something one should reduce or be reductionistic about, the Christ is a gestalt, is an overarching dimensional paradigm. Consider Paul's reference to Christ being IN us, and we being SONS of God, and as being joint heirs with Christ. Furthermore, a close reading can reveal that suffering is not necessarily the wages for sin, but that it is the birth pangs of the universe. Now more from St. Paul:

> However, we speak wisdom among them that are perfect; yet not the wisdom of this age, nor of the princes of this age, that come to nothing; But we speak the wisdom of God in a mystery, even the hidden wisdom, which God ordained before the ages unto our glory; [...]
>
> Now we have received, not the spirit of the world, but the Spirit who is of God; that we might know the things that are freely given to us of God. [...]
>
> [...] He that is spiritual judgeth all things, yet he himself is judged of no man. For who hath known the mind of the Lord, that He may instruct him. But **we have the mind of Christ**.[78] (Emphasis added).

"Speak wisdom among them that are **perfect!**" Paul is writing that others have perfected themselves. What! You mean others have perfected themselves beside Jesus? Here again one may overlook the fact that perfectibility by others in additional to Jesus has and does occur. And yet when Jung speaks of Christ being a symbol of the self, and asserts that the Christ image is as good as perfect, while the archetype designates completeness and is far from being perfect;[79] so I will add that being whole and complete is in itself a certain perfection, which is just great. Or consider this passage, "Now you are Christ's body, and individually parts of it."[80]   Here are more additional scriptures:

> But now is Christ risen from the dead and become the first fruits of them that slept. For since by man came death, by man came also the resurrection of the dead. For as in Adam all die, even so in Christ shall all be made alive; But every man in his own order: Christ the first fruits; afterward they that are Christ's at his coming. Then cometh the end, when he shall have delivered up the kingdom to God the Father, when he shall have put down all rule and all authority and power. For he must reign, till he hath put all enemies under his feet. The last enemy that shall be destroyed is death. For he hath put all things under his feet. But when he saith all things are put under *him, it is* manifest that he is expected who did put all things under him. And when all things shall be subdued unto him, then shall the Son also himself be subject unto him that put all things under him, that **God may be all in all.**...
>
> Behold, I show you a mystery: We shall not all sleep, but we shall all be changed. In a moment, in the twinkling of an eye, at the last trump; for the trumpet shall sound, and the dead shall be raised incorruptible, and we shall be changed.   For this corruptible must put on incorruption, and this mortal must put on immortality. So, when this corruptible shall have put on incorruption, and this mortal shall have put on immortality, then shall be brought to pass the saying that is written, Death is swallowed up in victory.[81]   (Emphasis added).

Think of a torus, the shape of which is that of a doughnut or of an inner tube of a tire, that such a "circular solid" rotates, and as it does it goes in on itself yet extending and expanding. Think of this beyond mathematics and into botany, a torus is a receptacle which is where the sex organs are situated and in some plants can become part of the fruit itself; we realize that this receptacle receptor is receptive to receive a particular stimulus, initiates a change within itself and then transmits a message, which grows and purifies and sanctifies itself as it does grow.   And before long, like a seed germinating you witness the manifesting growth of the next generation of life such that you comprehend the All in All.   Now to continue with St. Paul:

> Therefore, if any man **be in Christ, he is a new creation**; old things are passed away; behold, all things are become new.   And **all things are of God**, who hath reconciled us to himself by Jesus Christ, and hath given to us the ministry of reconciliation; To wit, that God was in Christ reconciling the world unto himself, not imputing their trespasses unto them, and hath committed unto us the word of reconciliation.   Now, then, we are ambassadors for Christ, as though God did beseech you by us; we beg you in Christ's stead, be ye reconciled to God.   For he hath made him, who knew, no sin, to be sin for us, that we might be made the righteousness of God in him. [82]   (Emphasis added).

> We are God's work of art, created in Christ Jesus for the good works which God has already designated to make up our way of life. [83]

Jesus bore witness to the Christ power; that is why Paul writes the word <u>Christ</u> first, then <u>Jesus</u>.   For Jesus attuned himself to the identification of spirit, our true nature.   Spirit comes first, the Christ, and then secondarily comes the identification with a body - Jesus.   The same can be said for and about us, each one of us in our <u>own order</u>.   For we are coming to express this very way and to be able to say from the depths of our own Self-Realization that, "I am the way, the truth, and the life."   I cannot get to the Father except through the Christ in me.   Drawing from the light of Christ within, plus the example of Jesus, we too will do "the same works and greater far than" he, thereby expressing the spirit of the ever living and omnipresent Christ through our mind and body.   When Paul writes "created in Christ Jesus", he gives an excellent example of Jung's writings concerning manifesting instincts which express themselves through one individual and are only the partial manifestation of an instinctual substrate common to all men. This affirms that we have that "latent seed that corresponds to the prototype Jesus", emanating from the higher Christ within. This is the Redeemer archetype present within us all. Again remember the Principle of Correspondence - as above, so below.

> Now I rejoice in my sufferings for your sake, and in my flesh I am filling up what is lacking in the afflictions of Christ on behalf of his body, which is the church, of which I am a minister in accordance with God's stewardship given to me to bring to completion for you the word of God, the mystery hidden from ages and from generations past. But now it has been manifested to his holy ones, to whom God chose to make known the riches of the glory of this mystery among the Gentiles – **it is Christ in you, the hope for glory.** [84] (Emphasis added).

The Letter of Paul to the Colossians has so much to say I find it tempting to recite much of it here, but it will just have to suffice with the following and leave it to you the reader to go read it fully from your own Bible:

> But now you must get rid of all such things – anger, wrath, malice, slander, and abusive language from your mouth. Do not lie to one another, seething that you have stripped off the old self with its practices and have clothed yourselves with the new self, which is being renewed in knowledge according to the image of its creator. In that renewal there is no longer Greek or Jew, circumcised and uncircumcised, barbarian, Scythian, slave and free; but **Christ is all in all!**[85] (Emphasis added).

Now what more needs to be said! Not another verse, or half verse, much less a word needs to be added to this most basic truth. So I have to address those who call themselves Christians to not deny this truth any longer, please stop opposing this fact. You are worthy; you are not wretched, your true self is not flawed, nor are you guilty of some nebulous sin, unless you are teaching that you are separate from the Trinity, and in that case just stop it because in reality we are not, rather we are one. If Jesus and Paul use the word <u>Christ</u> and not the word <u>Jesus</u>, if Christ is "all in all" then that means EVERYTHING IN ALL of YOU, then every cell, tissue, organ, and every system of this body and of this mind is THE CHRIST. If Christ is all of me, then I AM simply the very expression of the Living God. It's **IN YOU, It's IN ME, and It's IN US. It's ALL AROUND US, IT BINDS AND PENETRATES US.** Can we really be with this? Therefore, it doesn't matter what any half-conscious person is going to say regarding our connection to the Fatherhood of God; we are at one with God and with Jesus, with absolutely no separation. But telling someone this most likely won't do. The person will have to be asked: what do you have to say about Paul's writing that, "Christ is all in all"? Which is to say Christ **IS EVERYTHING IN ALL OF YOU**? This is our Identity.

Also, if any professing Christian gets mad at this perspective, then he ought to quit calling God "Father," because the Gospel of John, speaking of Jesus in chapter 5:18 says, "...the Jews tried all the more to kill him, because he not only broke the sabbath but he also called God his own Father, making himself equal with God."[86] Remember, Jesus said God is Our Father! Does this imply equality? I am not trying to be arrogant about this, but rather truthfully consider what it means to put on the mind of Christ.

There is a question that often arises in certain circles, 'Do you accept Jesus as your personal savior?' This relationship is contingent upon an **<u>internal decision</u>** (your acceptance) and not per se on Jesus' action. Jesus could have done what he did, but if one doesn't accept His efforts, then what does it mean? Nothing. So we have our own very big role in the whole plan of salvation. Remember as was cited in the beginning of this paper, "by patient endurance you will save your lives." Here are more readings from Galatians that affirm Christ is the power and Jesus is the pattern:

> Wherefore, the law was our schoolmaster to bring us unto Christ, that we might be justified by faith. But after faith is come, we are no longer under a schoolmaster. For ye are all the sons of God by faith in Christ Jesus. For as many of you as have been baptized into Christ have put on Christ. There is neither Jew nor Greek, there is neither male nor female; **for ye are all one in Christ Jesus**. And if ye be Christ's, then are ye Abraham's seed, and heirs according to the promise.
> Now I say *that* the heir, as long as he is a child, differeth nothing from a servant, though he be lord of all. But is under tutors and governors until the time appointed of the father. Even so we, when we were children, were in bondage under the elements of the world. But, when the fullness of the time was come, God send forth his Son, made of a Woman, made under the law, to redeem them that were under the law, that we might receive the adoption of sons. And because ye are sons, God hath sent forth **the Spirit of His son into your hearts**, crying, Abba, Father. Wherefore, thou are no more a servant, but a son; **and if a son, then an heir of God through Christ.**[87] (Emphasis added).

> Stand fast, therefore, in the **liberty** with which Christ hath made us free, and be not entangled again with the yoke of bondage.... For, brethren, ye have been **called unto liberty**; only use not liberty for an occasion to the flesh, but by love serve one another. For all the law is fulfilled in one word, even in this: Thou shalt love thy neighbor as thyself. [88] (Emphasis added).

> I am crucified with Christ: nevertheless I live; yet not I, but Christ liveth in me; and the life which I now live in the flesh I live by the faith of the Son of God, who loved me and gave himself for me.[89]

The New Scofield Reference Bible has as an introduction to this section of Gal 2:20 that reads, "The Christian life is the outliving of the in living Christ."[90] Does that explain it? Those who put together the Bible know what the differentiation is and St. Paul himself could not of and did not use the word Jesus living in him. Paul and the editors of the Holy Bible use the word <u>Christ</u>. Because of these Christ conscious men we have reason to rejoice, for it is our inheritance, the very glory to be revealed <u>In Us</u>, with the world eagerly awaiting God's Son's revelation and manifestation. For it is just as Paul writes in 1 Cor 2:7: "Rather, we speak God's wisdom, mysterious, hidden, which God predetermined before the ages for our glory."[91] We awaken to the Truth that our True Self is that of the Christ of God. We are the Sons of God, the heirs of God through Christ.

I have cited just a few quotations from Paul's epistles. In reading them for oneself, many more passages can easily be found that refer to the Christ as Consciousness, beyond the singular expression of Jesus, the usage which includes you. All of the gifts of the Father are our inheritance. He/She has given us the vision of Christ. As we accept these gifts, we accept Heaven. As Jesus stated in John 17:5, I ask the same; "And now, O Father, glorify thou me with thine own self with the glory which I had with thee before the world was."[92]

The Way, The Truth, and The Life

There is a scripture passage that I want to bring up that a fundamentalist would cite in order to build his/her case that only Jesus is the way. That passage is from the Gospel of John, Chapter 14, verse 6, and it reads: "Jesus said to him, 'I am the way and the truth and the life. No one comes to the Father except through me."[93]

Now I want to consider another statement of Jesus', one that I have already cited from John 5:30: "I can of my own self do nothing. As I hear, I judge; and my judgment is just, because I seek not mine own will, but the will of the Father who hath sent me." And also from chapter 8:28b: "...and *that* I do nothing of myself; but as my Father hath taught me."[94] Here we have two passages that are of someone who has a complete humbleness, yet the passage out of chapter 14 could be viewed as someone who is a total egomaniac.

The thesis of this manuscript is that what Jesus is implying is that he is speaking from the Christ Mind and not from the personality of the body, but nevertheless the body, matter, earth contains the divine seed of the third sonship. That at this point in his development Jesus had totally identified with the Christ power, the anointed one, or that which without Him was not anything made that was made. That power ran through Jesus as it runs through us. So, only through the Christ power can one get to the Father. Thankfully, that Christ is within. Therefore if we hear anyone saying, lo he is here, or lo he is there, we don't have to go running after any external messiah. And it is right for us to affirm this very statement our self from our own Christ within us that I am the way, the truth, and the life. Another thing to be thankful for is that Jesus did achieve Christhood, and for that accomplishment he is a model of the way.

Developing the Christ Consciousness

Donald Curtis, in his book <u>Finding the Christ</u>, asserts that the Christ consciousness develops in a four step progression; 1) Jesus, 2) Jesus Christ, 3) Christ Jesus, and 4) Christ. Curtis makes some key points:

> Jesus is our first stage of spiritual adjustment, attunement, and development: Jesus, the man. [...]This is the stage in which we come to recognize ourselves as innately spiritual beings. But we are still very much in the world at this level. [...]
> Jesus Christ: Jesus, the man; Christ, the Son of God. We put these two names together in describing our unfoldment because we are both. We do not deny our humanhood [...], but we overcome [...] by establishing the freedom of Truth within us. […] This realization opens up ever greater opportunities and spiritual vistas for us. [...]
> The third level of development is Christ Jesus wherein

the spiritual comes first. We aspire to the point where we always give Spirit priority in our lives. [...]

The Christ is our true spiritual identity [...] When we acknowledge prayerfully, "You are the Christ, the Son of the living God" (Matt. 16:16) we are recognizing that universal inner presence of Spirit, the eternal Self, the reality of our being. Every one of us is the human expression of the Christ.[95]

This quote from Dr. Curtis amply describes the evolutionary process that we as humans go through in our own process of attaining enlightenment. Our True Self is the expression of God, which is the Christ. Let us then reform our lives, as John the Baptizer would say, and do so that the structure and shape of it bespeaks of us being in the operating mode that we are cognizant that God's reign is at hand, while we function as God's hands on earth. Or it could be said that we should repent, that is make a change in our lives for the better away from missing the mark or sinning (causing intrapsychic splits) and toward being and getting on the correct path of life that heals such splits within ourselves (causing redemption).

A Paradigm Shift

It is very wonderful that when researching a topic that one comes upon other written material that further supports the given topic, as if being attracted to it like an electromagnet; in a word - serendipity. The Coming of the Cosmic Christ, by Matthew Fox is the case in point coupled with this paper's thesis. *"Part III: From the Quest of the Historical Jesus to the Quest of the Cosmic Christ – A Paradigm Shift for Western Religion"* is most pertinent for our discussion now, Fox writes:

The Cosmic Christ is not a doctrine that is believed in and lived out *at the expense of the historical Jesus.* Rather, a dialectic is in order, a dance between time (Jesus) and space (Christ); between the personal and the cosmic; between the prophetic and the mystical. The dance is a dance away from anthropocentrism.

Nevertheless, in calling for a paradigm shift in theology and religion itself we are not talking about an easy change of consciousness or a simplistic change of agenda. To move from a 'personal Savior' Christianity-which is what an anthropocentric and antimystical Christianity gives us – to a 'Cosmic Christ' Christianity calls for *metanoia*, a change of perspective by all those who do theology and by those schools which claim to teach theology. It will no longer be possible to teach theology without art as meditation, without spiritual disciplines that are grounded in the body and that arouse the imagination, as an integral part of the curriculum. Just as science has its laboratory hours for teaching the methods of scientific inquiry, so too theology requires laboratories in painting, clay, ritual, massage, and music to teach the art of mystical development. Churches and synagogues require laboratories of prayer where the "prune brain" that the right lobe has become can be watered, nourished, and developed. The Cosmic Christ cannot find a home in a left-brain setting alone. No exclusively left-brained individual or institution, whether of education or of worship, can welcome the Cosmic Christ.[96]

Being Born Again

Being *born again* really should mean putting on the Mind of Christ as the many passages of Paul instructs us to do (Christ Consciousness); which is putting aside the old self and putting on the new self created in his image. It's not just going to be saying that Jesus is this, that or another, and making him responsible for everything; and that we can just let the world just go down the proverbial drain because Jesus is going to come and rapture us. It means that we take on all the things that Jesus was about and claim them for ourselves, in a very humble yet matter of fact reality. If we are **_one_** as Jesus teaches, and that is what the Logos teaches, then what else can one conclude when you contemplate Oneness and thereby identify with and ultimately embrace the same assertions as Jesus because of the Christ within. It's not robbery.

A Poem: The Land of Alchemy

Welcome to the land of Alchemy
Here we call forth and attune ourselves
To the objective, autonomous Psyche.
Engage in that internal inquiry,
So as to have that personal discovery of thy True Self.

Take your *prima materia* and extract from it *cogitatio.*
Turn the lead of despair and depression into that Philosophical
Gold; that is redeem the Soul, your Soul,
That archetypal God-image, which is hidden in matter.
Logos is buried in Eretz; Thy will be done in Earth.
To bring forth the creative immanence which is in us,
Is the absolute function of every human being.
That integrated whole Being waits to be expressed.
Hu-man, enter into that which transcends uniqueness and
Unitemporalness, and contemplate being universal and eternal.

Cognition, that universal physical principle,
In that it has physical effects,
Is that uniquely human capacity
That lets you know that thou are
Created in the image and similitude of YHVH.

And the winds blow across the face of it's very Self
And separates the waters from the earth.
Creating a space for the Incarnatio: for the human,
For you man, to come into existence, so as to bear witness
And act as an agent for the Christ Consciousness.

And as the elements are separated the ego feels separate,
Yet remember, you are more than an ego;
You are one individual, yet you are the many collective.
And as the opposites are reconciled within thy Self
You create a *Coniunctionis,* a sacred marriage, that brings forth
The radiance that fills us with the Love for Wisdom.

Chapter 3

The Continuing Revelation

In the continual unfolding of truth in manifestation, and of witnessing to the ever present reality of God, I relate to and write of the truth as it has been revealed to me. The truth, the continual revelation of that Universal Intelligence, Dynamo, and Energy that we call God speaking to us, His/Her children, in the present day is certain. That God reaches out to His children beyond manmade religious boundaries to those that are faithful. Now while I am not a member of this church, nor am I even necessarily advocating joining this or any church, because I am ultimately for freedom of thought, so what I am making reference to is <u>The Book of Mormon</u>, plus another book from The Church of Jesus Christ of Latter Day Saints, <u>Doctrine and Covenants</u>. These books, like the Bible, like Jung, Hall, Errico, and Fox, and <u>A Course in Miracles</u>, speak of the universality of the Christ, and of our Self as the Christ. In 3 Nephi we find this statement:

> And for this cause (desiring to speedily come unto Christ in thy Kingdom) ye shall have fullness of joy; and ye shall sit down in the kingdom of my Father; yea your joy shall be full, even as the Father hath given me fullness of joy; **and ye shall be even as I am, and I even as Father;** and the Father and I are one.[97] (Emphasis added).

How clear it is that Godhood has been extended to us Sons of God, who possess the Christ Consciousness. Similarly, as I have written a number of times already, as the Gospel of John (1:3-4) says, "Through Him all things came into being, and apart from Him nothing came to be. Whatever came to be in Him found life, life for the light of men," <u>Doctrine and Covenants</u> has scriptures in Section 88 which speak of the Light of Christ as, "The light which is in all things, which giveth life to all things, which is the law by which all things are governed,...who is in the midst of all things."[98]   To further this knowing, verse 6 says, "He that ascended up on high, as also he descended below all things, in that he comprehended all things, that he might be in all and through all things, the light of truth."[99]   Verses 7-12 speak of the Light of Christ that is in all, as all, and the power by which it was created (the sun, stars, the earth, all space, and the light that enlightens your eyes and quickens our understanding). Therefore, it is true, for our own "celestial glory," that we too shall "comprehend all things" because "we shall be even as He is," taking on the I Am consciousness.[100] This sharing of the kingdom, as Jesus teaches, is the way of teaching that the Sons of God are brothers of equality. And it is so even now.

      Doctrine and Covenants is great supportive scripture attesting to our innocence: "Every spirit of man was innocent in the beginning; and God having redeemed man from the fall, men became again, in their infant state, innocent of God."[101] It is good to know that in the presence of Universal God Intelligence, we, His/Her children, are truly innocent - sinless and guiltless. Now that we know this is so, let's be and act such that we stay this way.

Add to this a Word from Science

      This is reason for gratitude and experiencing joy, for after all we have received "a fullness of joy" due to our inseparable connection with the elements as spirit.[102] As I was writing in the previous chapter about the kingdom of heaven being likened to a field in the section of *The Christ: A Psychological Image of Wholeness,* this would be a good time to bring up the idea and fact of the Zero Point Field, which is referred to as *the vacuum* by physicists and is one enormous reservoir of energy such that this ground state field of energy continually interacts with all subatomic matter causing random fluctuations of energy without any readily seen cause.

In her book, <u>The Field: The Quest for the Secret force of the Universe</u>, Lynn McTaggart writes of the Zero Point Field as:

> [...] At our most elemental, we are not a chemical reaction, but an electric charge. Human beings and all living things are a coalescence of energy in a field of energy connected to every other thing in the world. This pulsating energy field is the central engine of our being and our consciousness, the alpha and the omega of our existence.
>
> There is no 'me' and 'not-me' duality to our bodies in relation to the universe, but one underlying energy field. This field is responsible for our mind's highest functions, the information source guiding the growth of our bodies. It is our brain, our heart, our memory – indeed, a blueprint of the world for all time. The field is the force, rather than germs and genes, that finally determines whether we are healthy or ill, the force which must be tapped in order to heal. We are attached and engaged, indivisible from our world, and our only fundamental truth is our relationship with it. 'The field,' as Einstein once succinctly put it, 'is the only reality.' [103]

The idea and fact here is that underlying the seeming separation and diversity of existence there is a unifying reality, i.e., all things are one. As evolution of consciousness continues it is comprehended that the scientist is not just a separate ego detached and isolated in a research lab; the objects that we take in through our sensory receptors - eyes, ears, and so forth - we eventually perceive at a certain level as *connected* to us, despite the space that exists between the subject and the object. The object is a subject is an object. Objects in the world are manifestations from the absolute, undifferentiated reality that have emerged from the Field, and without the pre-existence of the Field we couldn't even come into being because the Field had to be in place before we could emerge in it. We have to grasp with our mind's eye to see that energy fields bind and hold atoms and elements together. Those schools of thought such as British empiricism and its associations such as positivism, materialism, and reductionism have had their bottom fall out from under them because they were asserting that we were born a blank slate and that all knowledge came in through the senses. Yet now we know that matter is energy bound within fields, and the fields are an effect of Consciousness out picturing itself.

Let's Enter into Our Exaltation

Another verse from <u>Doctrine and Covenants</u> speaks of our shared godhood, for it attests to other men who have already attained such a condition:

> Abraham [...] abode in my law; as Isaac also and Jacob did none other things than that which they were commanded; and because they did none other things than that which they were commanded, they have entered into their exaltation, according to the promises, and sit upon thrones, and are not angels but are gods.[104]

If ever there is a perspective befitting of the thesis presented here, it is the Unitarian Universalists idea that: "We believe in the never-ending search for Truth. If the mind and heart are truly free and open, the revelations which appear to the human spirit are infinitely numerous, eternally fruitful, and wondrously exciting."

Another quote from the <u>Doctrine and Covenants</u> because it so perfectly exemplifies the whole purpose of the effort of this paper:

> And again we bear record - for we saw and heard, and this is the testimony of the gospel of Christ concerning them who shall come forth in the resurrection of the just. They are they who received the testimony of Jesus. [...]
> They are they into whose hands the Father has given all things - They are they who are priests and kings, who have received of his fullness, and of his glory; [...]
> Wherefore, as it is written, they are gods, even the

sons of God - Wherefore, all things are theirs, whether life
or death, or things present, or things to come, all are theirs
and they are Christ's, and Christ is God's. [105]

We are the recipients of God's fullness and glory. It's the
gospel of Christ, the testimony of Jesus, we are the heirs, we
are Christ's and Christ is God's; what more needs to be said?

What I will say is that we contemplate the word
exaltation, and that we experience the high feelings of intense
joy and well-being and pride and elation; of being elated
because we comprehend that we are an aspect of, a member of
a Universal Cosmic creation with our own creative
characteristic capacities. And so with awe I give thanks for our
elevated status and rank within this creative universe,
knowing that I too am to do *art* in the heavens and on/in
earth, and that I am earth and in earth is lodged a third of the
divine sonship.

A Poem from a Christian Mystic

Again, referring to the <u>Teachings of the Christian Mystics</u>,
which is a real wonderful compilation of writings in an
anthology of the Christian mystical tradition, so much of it is
compelling and makes me want to say, "Please read and
contemplate these sayings (thought forms)!" Of all the worthy
excerpts of the various mystics of and from the Christian faith
I will cite Saint Teresa of Avila, with a piece entitled *Envoi:
You Are Christ's Hands:*

> Christ has no body now on earth but yours,
>   no hands but yours,
>   no feet but yours.
> Yours are the eyes through which is to look out
>   Christ's compassion to the world;
> Yours are the feet with which he is to go about
>   doing good;
> Yours are the hands with which he is to bless men now.[106]

Chapter 4

The Collective Christ – A Collective Messiah

In further support of the truth that the Christ is not only individual but is also collective, and that we ourselves are in a very real way the very saviors that we seek, meaning that the messiah is not entirely an entity outside of ourselves, is found in Erich Fromm's book <u>You Shall Be As Gods</u>. In chapter four, "The Concept of History," Fromm writes that in the prophetic (biblical) and the rabbinic (post biblical) literature:

> The end of the days,' or 'the messianic time'...is not a state predetermined by God or the stars; it will not happen except through man's own effort. The messianic time is the historical answer to the existence of man. He can destroy himself or advance toward the realization of the new harmony. Messianism is not accidental to man's existence but the inherent, logical answer to it - the alternative to man's self-destruction.[107]

This sounds as lot like Luke 21:19 (by your perseverance you will save your lives). Fromm teaches that "man makes his own history," and that God does not interfere by "an act of grace or by coercion; he does not change the nature of man or his heart." The messianic time is the next step in history, not its abolition. The messianic time is the time when "man will have been fully born." At this point *man* will be at home again, he will be at-one, and be so in the world. In Fromm's teaching, the messianic time is:

> "[…] not brought about by an act of grace or by an innate drive within man toward perfection. The messianic time is brought about by the force generated by man's existential dichotomy: being part of nature and yet transcending nature; being animal and yet transcending nature."[108]

Conflict and suffering are generated by this dichotomy, and so it is by this perplexing existence that humanity is driven, which provides the activity, to resolve this conflict. Becoming fully human and achieving at-onement are the incentives that provide the direction of this activity (the drive). In this next step in history - that of achieving at-onement and becoming fully human - harmony is restored between humanity and nature.

Accepting the At-onement

Achieving at-onement or healing the thought of separation begins by accepting It (being at-one with the Source) to begin with. And so we accept and acknowledge this reconciliation of humanity to and with God, this connection or original condition. Therefore, "the messianic time is the return to innocence and at the same time is no return at all, because it is the goal toward which man strives after having lost his innocence."[109] This return of our "innocence" is not one of naivety or ignorance but rather one of healing intrapsychic splits and realizing guiltlessness. In this we realize that our essential nature has not been corrupted, and it is as it always has been, as Genesis describes it, "good," and that there exists an original blessing which we finally perceive. Thus we remember our image and likeness and our True Self.

The Messianic Time: The Prophetic or Biblical Concept

The prophetic literature or the biblical concept of the messianic time instructs that the coming of the "messiah" or "the anointed one" will manifest in different ways. The "saviors" to the prophets Amos, Ezekiel, and Obadiah, as related by Fromm, "are only a collective messiah, and not an individual one." However, in some of the prophets: Nahum, Zephaniah, Habakkuk, Malachi, Joel, and Daniel, there is no human messiah at all; the Lord alone is the redeemer.[110] These two descriptions of the coming of the messiah are not, in an absolute sense, contradictory. The reason they complement each other is that, with the acceptance of the at-onement, we realize that humanity expresses as God, and remember that "God be all in all," that through God all things came to be and that apart from Him nothing came into existence. As Jesus said it, "I cannot do anything on my own; I judge as I hear, and my judgment is just, because I do not seek my own will but the will of the one who sent me."[111] Further, in accepting or welcoming the messiah we are "welcoming Him who sent" the anointed one, implying that Natural forces are God forces; again it is "God" in the form of a human, just like Paul writes about Jesus, which is the expression of God on earth; and it is in the acceptance of the at-onement that we can begin to call ourselves by the name of the Lord, which is Christ. This is true Christianity. Now with this realization the transformation begins, because of our "new" perceptual view that we envision ourselves as whole and complete, which is perfect, as in its perfectly fine or sufficient, just as the Holy Spirit sees us. For now we are actualizing the perfection of our own Christhood, for we now have the vision of Christ. Christ is not only the end, he is the means; he is not only the objective, he is the process as well.

Remember too, from the Analytical or Depth Psychology view, the psyche is the sacramental container, therefore numinous or divine encounter experiences are located forth-rightfully and profoundly within ourselves; hence the Self, i.e., the messiah/Christ, which cannot be distinguished from the God image, is the Autonomous Objective Personality taking the redeeming action, even though it may look like some regular man or woman.

When we view ourselves with the eyes of the Holy Spirit, it is not that we deny ever experiencing frustrations, anger, let-downs, or anything that is generally labeled as negative, but what we do deny is the absolute hold of these experiences on us and in so doing we release them so that we can get on with actualizing that "positive" potential Energy. Furthermore, because of the love for God we keep in mind that all things work for good, therefore we stay attentive to the ongoing communication between the Holy Spirit and ourselves to know how to be and what to do.

We have realized that humanity is the expression of God on earth and we have accepted the at-onement, and yet to Fromm, we actualize this or, "become fully human, fully born" by developing the specifically human capabilities of *love and reason*, and it is in this way that we truly "shall be as gods", i.e., creators. Yes, we call ourselves by the name of the Lord, so that we can be transformed. We take on the I Am consciousness, for we must and do assert and affirm our likeness with and as God because this is our very image - the creations are indistinguishable from the Creator. In Christian terms we totally identify with the Christ, seeing the face of Christ in all of our brothers and sisters, so as to remember God. By identifying with Christ, we are no longer mere men but are glorified humanity. In Fromm's words:

> Seen from the standpoint of biblical philosophy, the process of history is the process in which man develops his powers of reason and love, in which he becomes fully human, in which he returns to himself. [...] In the process of history man gives birth to himself. He becomes what he potentially is, [...] that man would become like God himself.[112]

The Messianic Time: Rabbinical/Post Biblical View

Moving to the rabbinical or post-biblical development of the Messianic Concept, we note two concepts that are considered the required conditions for the coming of the messiah. The first one is catastrophic conditions, in which these conditions get to such a high degree that, "men will repent and thus be ready."[113] The second concept is that, "the messiah will come not after catastrophes, but as the result of man's own continuous improvement."[114]   It is this second idea that places the responsibility for salvation in our hands - or more accurately in our attitudes, decisions, mindsets, and the subsequent behaviors that result from our living within the bounds of God's Law or even universal physical principles. This is so because it is our perception that will influence and determine behavior and experience, making salvation an ongoing living process that doesn't begin after we depart from this physical realm but very much includes this world. "Redemption depends on the process of perfection by the people themselves."[115]   Redemption and salvation depend on the factor of decision, not of time, so this makes today the Day of Judgment. Today, if you will hear The Voice, listen so as to return to your Source. The Voice says, 'You are a child of God and of Life Itself, an indispensable part of the Kingdom, and Heaven is your home, and it doesn't exclude you being in and on the Earth.'

Actually the Second Coming

The messiah has in fact come once. Further, what has to be realized is that as humanity continues to perfect (by accepting being whole and complete) itself one individual at a time by communing with the Tree of Life, and as we do so more collectively, the Second Coming happens. It happens because a significant number of people will have acknowledged what their True Self is, will have accepted the atonement, and will be living a Christ-centered and directed life. Even catastrophes will diminish. Of course, Jesus will be there, yet the Christ is here now, even as Jesus the Christ said, "Again, [amen,] I say to you, if two of you agree on earth about anything for which they are to pray, it shall be granted to them by my heavenly Father. For where two or three are gathered in my name, there am I in the midst of them."[116] Also, "…And behold, I am with you always, until the end of the age."[117]   What else could this be but awareness, a consciousness that Christ is present now? So the messiah isn't just in some external redeemer; the messiah is in all and is all of us.   In this way we are enraptured, for the Christ Consciousness descends upon us as if from a cloud and we are raised to Heaven's awareness. Salvation is contingent upon our beingness to do the right thing. Humanity is the Temple that has to be rebuilt; external temple building in any country is secondary to this. We are to build heaven on earth; God's will is to be done in earth (us) as it is in heaven.

Fromm cites evidence of the "Messiah within" idea as being present in the Hasidic movement within the Jewish tradition. Fromm quotes a Rabbi replying to a question:

> "The Messiah could come today without being proceeded by Elijah, if we ourselves prepare our hearts without troubling the Prophet to do it for us.   Let us make ourselves ready, then, to receive the Messiah any day by obeying the Voice of the Lord."[118]

One other example Fromm cites from the Hasidic movement:

> "That the messiah is by no means God, but utterly human, and that his coming is the result of the growing perfection of the people: Said the Stretiner: 'Each has within himself an element of the messiah which he is required to purify and mature. Messiah will come when Israel has brought him to the perfection of growth and purity within themselves.'"[119]

"Israel", while meaning one who contends until victorious, and its meaning can extend to mean the perfected individual or nation. Also, the word often comes across as sounding like "Is Real", so think of it as one has become "Is Real" in the sense that this human has achieved full Self-Realization. Again, the savior is paradoxically, totally divine and human, and is us, so let us resolve any intrapsychic splits and mature.

Said even another way by Andrew Harvey, the editor

of the anthology <u>The Teachings of the Christian Mystics</u>:

> The Second Coming will not, I believe, be in the return of Christ as a figure: that version perpetuates the old deification of Christ that has kept his force inert in history. The *real* Second Coming will be the birthing of Christ-consciousness in millions of beings who turn, the Father-Mother, towards the fire of love and take the supreme risk of incarnating divine love-in-action on Earth. This Second Coming could potentially alter the level of consciousness of the whole of humanity and initiate it into that mystical wisdom that it desperately needs if its problems are going to be solved.[120]

Again, let us give birth to the Christ within by first accepting it, in so doing we are no longer fallen, for we now accept the spirituality of a creation centered reality where we emphasize our original blessing and not some original sin.[121]

A Collective Christ/Messiah Action

If Jesus' teaching was a rejection of a military messiah, then what sort of Godly justice did he envision and teach? After all, the first generations of saints who picked up his teachings eventually helped put an end to the Roman Empire.

Now the Book of Moroni, in the <u>Book of Mormon</u>, 7:16 states, "The Spirit of Christ is given to every man, that he may know good from evil." Since all things came into being by Him and apart from Him nothing came to be, then it can be said that evil won't or can't exist absolutely or that evil is limited in its existence because "we know that all things work for good for those who love God, who are called according to his purpose," as Paul writes.[122] Very briefly, I am reminded of the story in Genesis of Joseph being sold into slavery into Egypt by his brothers, which one could judge that this is an evil act, and yet before too long Joseph is ruling the place; he forgives them and even saves them from a famine, all which proclaims a greater plan revealed by God.

It's obvious that we have been called; we then have to ask are we living according to His purpose? It also becomes, therefore, a question of perception as to what is Reality in the "eyes" (to and with the knowledge) of The All and to keep listening to the voice of the Lord, i.e., asks for the guidance of the Holy Spirit. Because if Christ is everything in all of us or is the All in All, it is our duty to look beyond the appearance of duality and thereby work for and call forth the Christ within, even if there is not one bit of empirical evidence to support that which is whole at the moment. Now knowing that everything and all people are in essence the expression of Christ (because all things are controlled and governed by the Light of Christ), we can do it. Some as of yet have not awakened to their innate godliness or their divinity, but it is the purpose of this writing to assert and affirm (take on the perceptual view of) humanity's original blessing and holiness and to help in the enlightenment or liberation of consciousness, because in so doing it just may be the very instance that brings us beyond critical mass and into a higher level of harmony.

In addition to practicing the Golden Rule of doing unto others as you would have them do unto you, the most potent example was and is of Jesus kicking the money changers out of the temple. And for the collective messiahship/Christ to act today would be to have a modern day kicking the money changers out of the temple of our nation and the world. Not that the money changers need a whip taken to them, but they do need to have the force of law brought on them. The way to do that is to model this action off of Franklin D. Roosevelt and his Banking Act of 1933, otherwise known as the Glass–Steagall Act, which separated legitimate commercial bank functions from speculative "investment" functions. The looters that are monetarists got their way in 1999 and had the Glass–Steagall law rescinded, which has been a lynchpin leading to the financial meltdown over the past four years. Under Glass-Steagall standards, all banking institutions are forced to choose between either commercial or investment banking. Productive functions of banks are federally protected and insured, while other worthless speculative activities are left out to wither and die. Under a New Glass-Steagall Bill into the trash will go derivatives, exotic financial instruments, mortgage backed securities, collateralized debt obligations, and carbon swaps; whereas the Department of the Treasury will protect infrastructure projects, loans to small businesses true mortgages, and pensions. Speculative activity is thrown out while commercial and deposit banking is protected. In President Roosevelt's inaugural address in 1933, the one where he speaks that "We have nothing to fear but fear itself", he also had this to say:

> [...] Practices of the unscrupulous money changers stand indicted in the court of public opinion, rejected by the hearts and minds of men.
> [...] their efforts have been cast in the pattern of an outworn tradition. Faced by failure of credit they have proposed only the lending of more money. Stripped of the lure of profit by which to induce our people to follow their false leadership, they have resorted to exhortations, pleading tearfully for restored confidence. They know only the rules of a generation of self-seekers. They have no vision, and when there is no vision the people perish.
> The money changers have fled from their high seats in the temple of our civilization. We may now restore that temple to the ancient truths. The measure of the restoration lies in the extent to which we apply social values more noble than mere monetary profit.
> Happiness lies not in the mere possession of money; it lies in the joy of achievement, in the thrill of creative effort. The joy and moral stimulation of work no longer must be forgotten in the mad chase of evanescent profits. These dark days will be worth all they cost us if they teach us that our true destiny is not to be ministered unto but to minister to ourselves and to our fellow men.[123]

It's time to act collectively as such a wise president to save our nation and civilization again from those who are deliberately looting the national treasury. It is time for the last vestige of a monetary empire to be finally defeated; a collective Christ/Messiah action can put an end to it. We are not picking up arms, but rather a pen to pass, more accurately repass, legislation to secure and promote the general welfare.

As of this writing in June 2011 there is a bill in Congress, H.R. 1489: The Return to Prudent Banking Act of 2011, which would revive Glass-Steagall and repeal sections of the Gramm-Leach-Bliley Act; this is the type of thing to do.

In speaking of a collective Christ action in the vein of Jesus' cleansing the temple, an interesting book, <u>The Urantia Book</u>, asserts that Jesus didn't act alone on that day the temple was cleaned of the money-changers. How those commissioned to put this book together came to depict what happened in the temple that day I can't confirm or deny, but nevertheless, I like what is asserted and will therefore use it as an affirmation and visualization for our purposes today, which is to say that Jesus "was not alone in resenting this profanation of the temple," that *common people* too "heartily resented this profiteering desecration of their national house of worship."[124] As the story goes:

> [...], Jesus stepped down from the teaching platform and, going over to the lad who was driving the cattle through the court, took from him his whip of cords and swiftly drove the animals from the temple. But that was not all; he strode majestically before the wondering gaze of the thousands assembled in the temple court to the farthest cattle pen and proceeded to open the gates of every stall and to drive out the imprisoned animals. By this time the assembled pilgrims were electrified, and with uproarious shouting they moved toward the bazaars and began to overturn the tables of the money-changers. In less than five minutes all commerce had been swept from the temple.[125]

The point is that, we have to act for social justice; it's not going to work to say Jesus is going to come back and do it for us.

Rather we must use examples of great leaders that have come before us, be it Jesus, or Abraham Lincoln, Gandhi, or Franklin Roosevelt as inspiration to move us into action to achieve what they did in their day to help put an end to empire, slavery and fascism, i.e., their fights with the money changers. As for Lincoln and FDR, by promoting the general welfare by issuing public credit for productive purposes, putting the money changers in their place, and building on a mass scale infrastructure projects. The things that a true nation-state republic is suppose to do for its citizenry. Furthermore, it's time to nationalize the Federal Reserve and bring it under the United States Treasury as the National Bank of the United States, such that the US government functions as its own bank as it has before; and whereas Webster G. Tarpley has said it is "no longer the preserve of unelected an unaccountable cliques of incompetent and predatory bankers."[126] Economist and statesman Lyndon H. LaRouche, Jr. has this to say about this subject:

> All of European history, including European civilization's unfolding in the America's, is characterized by a single principle of conflict, a conflict between *republicanism,* on the one side, and *oligarchism,* on the other. [...] the only real issue within European history as a whole, has been the conflict between the *republican* followers of Solon (638-558 B.C.), Socrates (469-01 B.C.), and Christ, on the one side, and the opposing usury-ridden heritage of Babylon, Canaan, and pagan Roman.[127]

Andrew Harvey, the editor of the anthology <u>The Teachings of the Christian Mystics</u>, has this to say about the initiative that is the scope of the undertaking of the work of the Christ:

> At the core of Christ's enterprise is an experience of this fire and the revolutionary passion of charity that blazes from it. This passion, as Christ knew and lived it, cannot rest until it has burnt down all the divisions that separate

one human heart from another and so from reality. No
authority except that of the Divine, is sacred to it; no
dogma, however hallowed, that keeps oppression of any
kind alive can withstand the onslaught of its flame. All of
human experience, personal and political, is arraigned and
exposed by it. It demands of everyone who approaches it
a loving and humble submission to its fierce, mind and
heart shattering power and a commitment to enact its laws
of radical compassion and hunger for justice in every
arena. Its aim is the irradiation of all of life with holy and
vibrant energy and truth, so that as many beings as
possible can live, here on earth and in the body, in a direct
relationship with God, each other, and nature, in what
Saint Paul unforgettably calls "the glorious liberty of the
children of God."[128]

I think this statement should make it very clear that the
assertions being made in this writing is not for the purpose of
being a pompous, arrogant egomaniac to claim that we are
equals with Jesus, far to the contrary, this realization makes it
extremely awing, demanding great presence of mind that I am
being aware of doing our Father's business.

Of course another type of collective Christ action
would be that of teaching that all things are one because
teaching oneness is what the Logos teaches. So if you are
teaching oneness, then you are acting as the Logos, which
would be following in the steps of Jesus, who attained
Christhood. Now it's our own turn to do what he did.

Integrating the Shadow of our Self

Edward Schillebeeckx writes that the historical point of
Jesus' Temple cleansing was "a prophetic act, intended by
Jesus to engender penitence and the conversion of Israel in the
'latter days'."[129] The only way to have this conversion or
radical change of heart (a *metanoia*), and if we are to make any
progress on this good versus evil issue, and which it is being
asserted that the money changers are and imperialism is evil,

then it requires, in view of the analytical or depth psychology perspective to consider these money changers and imperialists out to be the shadow aspects of our self. If the Christ/Self be the all in all, and the Light of Christ is the law by which all things are governed, then we have to view these people as the shadowy, dark character of our self as much as it would be tempting to say otherwise and deny it. And to the extent that we individually and collectively play in their Great Game we are really a part of them. The effort here is to not split-off the shadow (the evil aspects) of our self by way of repression and disavowal, but to integrate the other aspects of the total personality, which means we are viewing this situation psychologically and not exclusively dogmatically.[130]

Here we have to now remember as stated in the *A Discrimination of Opposites* subsection in Chapter 1, that the self isn't solely good and spiritual, which makes the shadow not as dark. So let's consider a few more scripture passages: "The Lord has made everything for his own ends, even the wicked for the evil day" (Proverbs 16:4); and Isaiah (45:7) "I form the light and create the darkness, I make well being and create woe; I, the Lord, do all these things." And it is worth noting that in the Catholic Study Bible that the footnote for this Proverb verse reads, "Even the wicked, in their punishment, cannot escape glorifying God's justice." While this Isaiah verse footnote reads, "Create woe: God permits evil for the sake of a greater good." With this in mind let's consider what Lionel Corbett has to say:

> [...} Unlike these strands of Hebrew mythology which acknowledge God as the author of evil, Christian theology insists that God, or Christ, is totally light. [...] Jung discusses the Antichrist as corresponding to the shadow of the Self. According to Jung (CW 9, ii, 76), in Christian dogma the archetype is 'hopelessly split into two irreconcilable halves, leading ultimately to a metaphysical dualism'. Dogmatic Christianity made the figure of Christ too sublimely light, so that the 'coming of the Antichrist is

an inexorable psychological law'. Hence all the fundamentalist worry about Satan as if that figure were a concrete external entity – material that has been forced into the unconscious is projected as it presses for recognition. Dogmatic attempts to maintain an image of the divine which is only light may be an attempt to bind the anxiety which results from the terrifying prospect that the divine may have a dark side, or that the 'devil' actually refers to an experiential aspect of the Self, and of course the self. We are logically forced into such a belief because of the dualistic perspective; if we view the Self or spirit as only good, then we tend to see the body, matter or nature as the carrier of the bad, which attitude has been part of the Christian heritage.[131]

Let us take a breath, be mindful and contemplate, and ask ourselves are we a money changer type that is ripping people off, or engaging in or going along with the imperialists such that we contribute to the terrorizing and suppression of humanity? If the answer is yes, then let us do penance so as to have *metanoia*, and therefore stop engaging in these shadowy behaviors.

God, the Good and the One

Let us now move into more philosophical grounds by asserting the idea of God as being identical with what is called the Good and the One, which is not my original idea but rather developed well by the Neo-Platonist philosopher Proclus, who was the head of the Philosophy School at Athens for fifty years during the 5th century AD. First of all, let's make clear what the word *identity* means. One definition reads, "The collective aspect of the set of characteristics by which a thing is definitively recognizable or known;" while another definition is "The quality or condition of being the same as something else." [132] So the objective here is to link and equate the set of characteristics of the Good and the One, quality and condition respectively, with God.

Proclus begins his 13th Proposition[133] thus: "Every good unifies what shares in it, all union is good, and the good is the same as the one." So begins our effort to enter into that Intellectual Yoga with the Divine through the Mind, which alone cognizes it and it is done for the purpose of being better, braver, and less idle. With that said, I think it's the most prudent to invoke a statement that is pure guidance by Dionysius the Areopagite:

> Leave the senses and the workings of the intellect, and all that the sense and the intellect can perceive and all that is not and that is; and through unknowing reach out, so far as this is possible, toward oneness with him who is beyond all being and knowledge. In this way, through an uncompromising absolute, and pure detachment from yourself and from all things, transcending all things and released from all, you will be lead upwards toward that radiance of the divine darkness that is beyond all beings…
>
> Emptied of all knowledge, man is joined in the highest part of himself, not with any created thing, nor with himself, nor with another, but with the One who is altogether unknowable; and in knowing nothing he knows in a manner that surpasses understanding.[134]

Now, the 13th Proposition of Proclus continues with:

> "If indeed the good brings about the wholeness of all beings, but what makes whole and holds together the being of each is the One, then the good for those it is present to brings completion as one and holds together according to the union." [135]

The next thing that seems intelligible (not merely sensible) would be to question two phrases of Proclus' proposition so far, that being: a) every good unifies *what shares in it,* and b) the good *for those it is present to* brings completion as one. This alerts us to the reality that this proposition can only be recognized through and with the mind and not by unguided senses. For the next sentence tells us, "And if the One is what brings together and holds together beings, *it perfects each according to its presence. Presence* and *present: Presence,* for our purposes, means "the state or fact of being present; and a person's manner of carrying himself, bearing; the quality of self assurance and confidence." *Present,* as a noun, means a "moment or period in time perceptible as intermediate between past and future, now." Though as an adjective *present* means "Being, pertaining to or occurring at a moment or period in time considered as the present, being at hand; and alert to circumstances, attentive."[136]

Why should I spend the time and space in defining these words? Because if *the One* perfects each according to their **attentiveness**, then achieving Oneness or union is contingent upon each of us availing ourselves to listening to the Logos just as Heraclitus taught. So, again, just what is the Logos that reveals to us that we are one? Cosmic reason? The Word? Yes, the historical Jesus was that, did achieve it, was declared it, and too the Logos was taught at least 500 years before Jesus, so the Logos is beyond his particular expression. Is it a rational force immanent in the world and within each individual human being?[137] When we listen to the Logos we grasp that intelligible element in the everyday world as being an image and similitude of *a pre-existing Divine Blueprint.* To say it another way, before anything manifested, there was a desire, a Divine Thought form, *Logos,* which was the creative source and then from the Pattern or Divine-blueprint, Logos (as Demiurge) called forth and then emanated out as the material world, which was the in-stroke and outstroke of creation. While Logos is transcendent, the mind being the bridge between the worlds, creates immanent proofs by applying meaning to phenomena, and as a result we have a cosmology that is *advaita,* a Sanskrit word meaning not dual or not two. The purpose of being a creative artist is to manifest ideas from the spiritual domain through the mind, via the use of imagination and into the material realm, for it is the mind that provides meaning to the forms. Since the Logos is Divine Thought-Form yet also manifestation in motion, then *according* *to reason* the way the mind operates both on perception and expression is in the form or structure of analogy or proportion.

Nicolaus of Cusa, the 15th Century Catholic Church Cardinal and major intellectual force that helped spawn the 15th Century Italian centered Renaissance, due partly to his application of the works of the Platonic Tradition, says this:

> [...] Man is a second god. For just as God is the Creator of real entities and of natural forms, man is the creator of rational entities and artificial forms. These are nothing other than similitudes of his intellect, just as the creatures of God are similitudes of the divine Intellect. Therefore, man has intellect, which is a similitude of the divine Intellect, in creating.
>
> Therefore, he creates something of the similitudes of the divine Intellect, so the extrinsic artificial figures are similitudes of intrinsic natural forms. Hence he measures his intellect through the power of his works and from this he measures the divine Intellect, as the truth is measured through its image.[138]

God is to man as man is to his (man's) works!

This, which is to show how one can speak of the Divine Interpenetrating the natural world, is the very purpose of Plato's *Timaeus*. This was to move us from a cosmology, to metaphysics to a pure theology, which is in the domain of philosophy, because this world is an image of something that "is a work of craft, modeled after that which is changeless and is grasped by a rational account, that is, by wisdom."[139] Practicing the art of philosophy is practicing being and doing loving things for the sake of wisdom. For the world and everything was to become LIKE Him. Therefore, Being is to becoming as Truth is to belief. This Likeness, which is the Supreme originating principle of the Universe, provides us with the basis for becoming the Other, it allows a transition, for the natural order that we experience is infused with a high order of intelligibility that can be expressed in analogies. If we are the Word made flesh, the incarnate Logos, then we are an analogue proportionate to the Logos. Therefore, we share in the Good and are unified in and with It; Proclus puts it "Then in this way unification is good for all."

Now, if that's the case and it is reasonable and intelligible to conclude that it is, then the next, fifth sentence of Proclus 13th proposition which reads, "But if union is in itself good, and the good is what unifies, the unqualified good and the unqualified One is the same, unifying and at the same time makes beings good," should not start with the word *but*. Rather the sentence should begin with the word *and* or *so* (as in *thus*) because the word "but" introduces a statement in opposition to what proceeds it; maybe though Proclus' original writing for this word could mean it but it just got lost in translation. Regardless, the statement that precedes it is not something to oppose, it is rather something in/of the desired condition, so it should read: *Thus* if union is in itself good, and the good is what unifies, the unqualified good and the unqualified One is the same, unifying and at the same time makes beings good. That is good.

Now let's put that aside to consider the analogy, *God is to Man as Man is to his works*. Does this not teach us of "an internal unity with a three-fold origin from its highest to its lowest term which includes the mean?"[140] Most certainly the highest term here - God - generates the most unitary potency of the three and communicates its unity to the entire order, unifying the whole from above while remaining independent of it.   If man, the mean term, reaches out toward both extremes, measures his intellect through the power of his works and from this he measures the divine Intellect, and man can work to produce Renaissance's, then man can get some idea as to the proportion that he is related to God. Then does not man's work, serving as the *limiting term,* produce a likeness and convergence in the whole order by returning again upon its initial principles and carries back to it the potencies which have emerged from it? Think of the torus (p. 62). By God, I think it does. Does this create a Oneness? Does this qualify as Good? Is this not what God does? Then we can most certainly reach and accept the conclusion of Proclus' last statement of the 13th Proposition that, "Goodness is union and union is Goodness and the Good is the One and the One is primarily the Good." And another word for all this is *cohere*, or having *coherence*, and being *coherent*.

Again I refer to Nicolaus of Cusa who confirmed this conclusion from his own work, *On the Hunt for Wisdom*:

> [...] For Beauty, which is that which it can be, is inaugmentable and irreducible, since it is at the same time the maximum and the minimum, is the actuality of all potential-to-become-beautiful, effecting everything beautiful, and as far as its capacity admits, conforming and converting it to itself.
>
> It is likewise with the Good, which is that which it can be, and with the True, with the Perfect, and everything which we laud in creatures. We see that when they are that which they can be, they are the eternal God in God. And hence we laud God as the efficient, formal and final cause of all beings.
>
> Above all it is still to be revealed, how the potential-to-become cannot be terminated by anything which follows it or that can become, but rather its beginning and end are the same. [141]

There is beauty in proportion and analogies, for in the study of the natural world we find the trace to and of the Divine, the Intelligible that orders the nature of things. That from pure energy comes the manifest realm in algorithmic fashion where **all goes in rhythm**. Or one can take analogies and create symbols or a mythos that bespeaks of Love and Logos, Eros and Agape, something with Being and Beingness, Good and Goodness, and not just see random particles without any intention behind them. In the Intelligible order is Beauty itself, which of course we participate in, are vitalized by, and in some mysterious way, perfected. The implication of reaching this conclusion is not simply to theorize about some existence by a pedant, but is something that requires one to take action, hence to *practice philosophy.*

Wrapped up in the idea of the Good is the notion of *Providence.* Providence is "the idea that something exists before the intellect, which is a Goodness that naturally flows out into the universe, which goes forth. Therefore it is in all."[142] Since it is in all and proceeds to everything then that sounds like something that promotes the *common good* or the *general welfare* and those who take up the promotion of the common good *participate* in creating and sharing the wealth. As a result these people, be it practicing philosophers or republic nation-state builders, act with a spirit of divinity for they are acting in such a way that doesn't deny the world but fulfills it. The realization is that the implications of such teachings as Proclus, Dionysius, Cusa, not to mention Plato's writings themselves are for another Renaissance in the making.

Contrary and in contrast to what was just written is the degradation, decay, and the "entropy" that has occurred over the past 40 years has happened because those imperialists and money changer types who have ascended into places of policy making have left out Classical Philosophical teachings and have promoted a financier-rentier, oligarchical, Malthusian structured system with their deindustrialization and deregulation of banking, who push privatizing the profits yet socializing the losses when their sorry schemes go bankrupt and they need to be bailed out by none other than the nation-state even though they constantly undermine it. Their floating exchange rate "system" is chaotic and increases disorder because it reflects an inherently unjust structure; they're monetarists and not physical economists, thankfully now the people from nation-states around the world are rejecting their anti-human plan, so their oligarchical tyranny is limited.

Let us briefly consider what Plato says through the figure of Socrates in Book I of the Republic, "for anyone who intends to practice his craft well never does or orders what is best for himself – at least when he orders as his craft prescribes

– but what is best for his subject."[143] This grand vision of art truly sets the stage for the practice of republican statecraft for the benefit of our fellow humanity. The art of ruling consists, at least in part, of making a diagnosis, putting forth a treatment plan, and providing any follow up program, be it physician, political office holder or any other craftsman. So the primary purpose of practicing an Art, as qualified by Socrates, is to benefit the subject, patient, or client without concern on the part of the craftsman for receiving any unjust or unwarranted benefit or profiteering.

In related matters and in regards to the issue at hand, Buckminster Fuller tells us that chemists had to recognize synergy because they found that elements did not act in isolation, but only in a complex association of "group proclivities." "Synergy reveals a grand strategy with the whole".[144] Furthermore, he speaks of the invisible revolution in the metallurgical, chemical and electronic arts which now makes it possible for humanity to do so much more with much less energy, material and time that literally everyone on earth can be taken care of at higher standards of living then previously ever known. Synergy reveals that entropy is not a universal law at all. He writes:

> All books on economics have only one basic tenet – the fundamental scarcity of life support… The supreme political and economic powers as yet assume that it has to be either you or me… It no longer has to be you or me. Selfishness is unnecessary and henceforth unrationalizable as mandated by survival. War is obsolete…Only ten years ago the more-with-less technology reached the point where it could be done…it is a matter of converting the high technology of weaponry to livingry".[145]

To achieve a win-win situation and create synergy, we have to overcome the hypnotic trance that there is scarcity. And too, know that science has time and again proved the Malthusians wrong. At this point in the evolution of humanity we have achieved the technological capacity to create a win-win situation for all. With this knowledge we can eliminate suffering. Abraham Maslow differentiates very well the cognitive attitudes, which takes us from one state of being to another, transforming a win-lose situation to a win-win one. Those attitudes are *deficiency-cognition* and *being-cognition*. Maslow writes that the Self-Actualizing adult:

> …knows the whole of the D-realm, the whole of the world, all its vices, its contentions, poverty, quarrels, and tears, and yet, is able to rise above them and to have the unitive consciousness in which he is able to see the B-realm, to the beauty of the whole cosmos in the midst of all the vices, contentions, tears and quarrels.[146]

Therefore, a world eagerly awaits some sound intelligible principles to be fully implemented on a grander scale then before, policies that are inclusive of promoting the common good; it means promoting a republican form of government over an imperial/empire model, so as to promote the full development of the citizenry. It means returning to the American system of political economy of Hamiltonian banking which establishes public credit for productive means and a National bank to promote the general welfare by building massive infrastructure projects, which is in contrast to the Anglo-Dutch Liberal system;[147] as in building a Lincoln type policy of Transcontinental Railway, as in doing one for our century in building the North American Water and Power Alliance project, which would be a 5o year building into the future project.[148] And now in 2011, after so many notable events, yet to cite them could really get beyond the scope of this intended writing, let me just cite the Preamble to the Constitution of The United States to remind us what the birth of the Republic that is the United States of America was and is intended to be for Americans and the cause for all mankind for that matter, particularly in light of this very section of contemplating oneness and the good:

> We the People of the United States, in order to form a more perfect Union, establish Justice, insure domestic tranquility, provide for the common defence, promote the general Welfare, and secure the Blessings of Liberty to ourselves and our Posterity, do ordain and establish this Constitution for the United States of America.

Suffice it to say that we have entered into the universal consciousness cycle within the Mayan Calendar Structure where Oneness is the coming understanding. Imagine, a sufficient number of people comprehending that we are connected at a level beyond the scope of our visual receptors and begin to act upon it, knowing that what I do to the least of my fellow humans I do to my Christ Self and to Christ Jesus.

The Real World Order

It is absolutely clear that the new harmony, the next step in history, is dependent on us, on our decision to choose life, liberty, justice, promotion of the general welfare, peace, and happiness; by comprehending the cosmological forces that we are in the milieu of and thereby harness those energies so as to advance into the new era, to become fully human by developing love and reason, to choose God and embrace our True Self, for after all we share the same One Will. It is by our own choice that "our heart changes," remembering now that our essence is that of what we call God. So ultimately, we do all that we can; we carry out all of the ideas that come to consciousness that are beneficial to all concerned. We act upon all of the ideas that are progressive toward the goal of harmony, and upon doing all that our reason has asked us to do, we release (or let go of) the results (effects) to the process of unfoldment, that is to say to God Himself that He and the Holy Spirit would take the last step, knowing that in the physical realm there is a time element involved. We would, in a word, *Trust*. For it is our duty, even our soul/sole purpose, to create heaven on earth. For Providence is calling.

Summary - Conclusion

I began this writing asserting in the Preface that the reason why I wrote this book was to get clear on this subject, therefore, I think it should be very clear at this point that "the Christ" is a title or office not solely confined to just Jesus. I have openly presented my religious opinions and I am thankful for the freedom of religious expression, and for living in a country that minimally promotes the freedom of religion and that there is no official state religion. For intellectual freedom and discovery of truth purposes I don't necessarily advocate joining any particular church, though it can be nice for gregariousness reasons.

In the Introduction I began to lay out the fact that the definition of the word "Christ" has and had evolved even within the span of time from the writings of the gospels to the writings of Paul's epistles. The purpose of this work has been to serve as a resource for those ready to accept that our ultimate Self is the Christ of God and that It is a Consciousness which is accessible to us; remember, we are an analogue of the Logos. Therefore, the Christ is not only an individual expression but is a collective manifestation as well, available to "every man that comes into this world" (John 1). With this we affirm our acceptance of the Christ as us, and we are empowered to become as children of God with all of the authority of the Holy Spirit. Certainly if we clothe ourselves with the "new self" that is created in God's likeness, then the dawn of a new age will happen in that individuals personal life, and if and as this new self is put on collectively, then a societal wide transformation will be witnessed to; remember we are to not only bear witness to but to act as an agent for the Christ consciousness. Therefore, let us create a space within ourselves for the Incarnation of the Christ within that it may be given birth.

The Jungian Analytical Psychology perspective

provided the foundation for this writing and for helping in the realization that the Christ is a symbol of the self, that the self is indistinguishable from the God image, and knowing our self to be whole and complete. Another purpose is to clarify that psychic processes in all individuals must be impersonal and conform to law, implying that what one has achieved by effort all can. Even Jesus taught this, and this is the very law that Paul writes of in his epistles when he writes "of the glory to be revealed through us." Therefore, another purpose is that we ourselves may awaken, be purified, and ascend, due to our own compelling nature to discriminate between opposites, by awakening "the latent seed" in us as Dr. Jung describes it. Because our true self is the Christ and thereby whole, we are naturally moving in the direction of unfoldment or completion; Fromm calls this movement our drive to be fully human by developing the capacities of love and reason.

  With our real, true, or ultimate self being whole and complete I also wanted to take this opportunity to encourage anyone who has been traumatized by whatever or however such that you are thinking and feeling fragmented in some fashion to seek out a way to resolve this conditioning so as to re-experience your wholeness, such as with a practitioner of Depth Psychology or of Emotional Freedom Techniques). Let it begin by accepting your wholeness as a given, and be healed by redeeming any intrapsychic splits for your inner Redeemer archetype will guide you.

  The extensive use of citing biblical passages, as stated before, is due to its place within our culture as "the word of God" and as such it supports fully the assertion what Jung asserts that Christ is a symbol of the self, especially when we comprehend what the divine blueprint that is the Logos. It should be obvious that the many scriptural passages cited in this writing bespeak of our oneness within the Trinity. Comprehending that the Christ is a psychological image of wholeness, which means that the seed of Christ is within you, should make it beyond any reasonable doubt that the

Kingdom of heaven is within you; it is as plain as that!

I, with genuine humbleness offered a New Penitential Rite that humanity may awaken to our original blessing and connection within YHWH, commonly called God, and that a paradigm shift in Western religion may take place. If we are to be the change we want to see in the world then may the revelations, the unveiling of the Sons of God be witnessed to this very day.

I have used other scriptures also in this writing to show that attaining the Christ is available to all humanity and not just confined to Jesus. What I am promoting is that it's time for us to accept and embrace our rise in rank and status within a Universal Creative Intelligence of which we are an analogue proportion of, therefore, let us enter into *that* elevated reality both with our thoughts and with the feeling that it is so and thereby act accordingly. Let us take the Vedanta definition of Self (Atman) which uses the word *saccidananda - being, consciousness, and bliss* - so as to awaken to the proper knowledge of our true Self and eliminate suffering due to ignorance and achieve liberation.

We, as beings created by an Omniscient Being, have access to all knowledge and thus we can know with certainty absolute truth. The knowledge of our ultimate Self as having been around since the beginning of creation and being eternal can be brought to awareness through the practice of meditation, or by just concentrated focus of your attention on a given subject matter and by asking Life the correct questions. We can also gain knowledge by utilizing the scientific method. This paper offers a means by which practical transcendence can occur by way of withholding judgment. I have done what I can to keep the notion of transcendence from being so mystical. Furthermore, this writing is offered as a vehicle of transformation in one's own life by shifting one's perceptual view away from being sinful (and therefore laced with guilt) and toward our original wholeness and innocence, because we are from God's stock and are created in the divine image. Let us identify with the Good and the One, which is God, and let us act in a way that promotes the general welfare. And engage in the talents we have been given by Life.

I have made an appeal to integrate the shadows of our self because at some point in this process discernments or judgments do have to be made as to the dark characteristics that are present. Because, remember psychologically (not theologically) these dark shadows are aspects of ourselves. Based on Jesus' kicking the money changers out of the temple I have pointed out both them and imperialists to be evil and to make sure we are not being duped or assisting in their efforts in any fashion, but rather working to end their reign. There can be and are many other dark shadowy characteristics that need to be healed on both individual and collective levels I have only really focused on these two factors due to the long term, civilization level affects and effects that they produce.

Lastly, this paper is a call for us to no longer be passive but rather to become activated in the process of achieving the New Harmony that has been started, thereby being response-able to the requisites of this harmony by developing love and reason. I have also offered an example of a collective Christ action, one that calls for *metanoia*. Overall this work is devoted to healing the thought of separation and thus creating an awareness of the at-onement. By simply asking Life imaginative and creative questions, and by engaging in the scientific method we will come to know the how and why of things (processes). By then asserting our reasoning mind and doing all of those actions that assure health, happiness, and success, we relax, knowing that these things are processes that have a time element to them. For when logic and reason have taken us as far as they can, we let go and trust the process of Life and the Holy Spirit as the Comforter, knowing that the enlightenment of reason and the transcendence of feeling are associations adjoined together within our ultimate, true Self. And while this writing surely isn't perfect, it is now complete.

References

Preface

[1] These four quotes: from <u>The Catholic Study Bible</u>, which uses the New American Bible, 1990, Oxford University Press, Inc

[2] Luke 4: 8, Holy Bible: <u>The New Scofield Reference Bible</u>, Authorized King James Version, Oxford University Press, 1967

Introduction

[3] The Catholic Study Bible

[4] Published by the Noorha Foundation, Santa Fe, New Mexico 87505

[5] Luke 17:20-21, <u>Holy Bible – From the Ancient Eastern Text</u>, George M. Lamsa , Harper Collins

[6] The Catholic Study Bible

[7] The Catholic Study Bible, p. 137.

Chapter 1

[8] Aion: Researches into the Phenomenology of the Self, 2nd edition, p. 31, Princeton, 1959,

[9] Ibid p. 31-33

[10] Ibid p. 22

[11] The Catholic Study Bible

[12] <u>Penguin Dictionary of Psychology</u>, 3rd Ed, p. 659, Penguin Books, 2001

[13] <u>Aion</u>, p. x.

[14] Ibid, p. x.

[15] Ibid, p. x.

[16] <u>The Book of Knowledge: The Keys of Enoch,</u> 3rd edition, p. 580, J.J. Hurtak, The Academy for Future Science, 1987.

[17] <u>Aion</u>, p. 34

[18] Catholic Study Bible, p. 426

[19] Ibid, p. 431

[20] <u>The Mystical Christ: Religion as a Personal Spiritual Experience</u>, p. 209-210, Philosophical Research Society, Inc. Los Angeles, 8th Printing 1999

[21] <u>The Presocratic Philosophers</u>, 2nd Ed., p. 187, Kirk, Raven, Schofield, Cambridge University Press 1983

[22] Ibid, p. 187-188

[23] Ibid, p. 187

[24] The Catholic Study Bible

[25] <u>Aion</u>, p. 7

[26] Ibid, p. 7

[27] Ibid, p. 8

[28] Ibid, p. 7

[29] Ibid, p. 67

[30] Ibid, p. 65

[31] Ibid, p. 64

[32] Ibid, p. 64-65

[33] Ibid, p. 66

[34] Ibid, p. 64-65

[35] Ibid, p. 63

[36] Ibid, p. 40

[37] Psalm 1:1-3, <u>Holy Bible – From the Ancient Eastern Text</u>, George M. Lamsa Translation

[38] Joe Dispensa, D.C., <u>Evolve Your Brain: The Science of Changing Your Mind</u>, p. 365,   Health Communications Inc., Florida 2007

[39] Ibid., p. 366

[40] <u>A Course in Miracles</u>, vol. 3, Manual for Teachers, p. 79-80, Foundation for Inner Peace, 1975

[41] <u>Teachings of the Christian Mystics,</u> Edited by Andrew Harvey, p. 92, Shambhala Boston/London, 1998

Chapter 2

[42] R. M. Bucke, <u>Cosmic Consciousness</u>, p. 2-7, Dutton & Co., 1969.

[43] Ibid, p. 62.

[44] <u>Let There Be Light: The Seven Keys</u>, 3rd Ed., pps. xxx, 189, Noohra Foundation, Santa Fe, New Mexico, 1996

[45] Ibid, pps. 187-189

[46] John 14: 20, Catholic Study Bible

[47] The Catholic Study Bible

[48] Commentary notes P. 1151, The New Scofield Reference Bible

[49] <u>Holy Bible – From the Ancient Eastern Text,</u> George M. Lamsa Translation, Harper San Francisco

[50] Footnote p. 169, Paramahansa Yogananda, <u>Autobiography of a YOGI</u>. Self-Realization Fellowship, Los Angeles, 1979.

[51] Princeton University Press, 1969

[52] The Catholic Study Bible

[53] 1 John 3: 9. Catholic Study Bible

[54] Romans 6: 6, 11, New Revised Standard Version, <u>The Complete Parallel Bible</u>, Oxford University Press, 1993.

[55] <u>The Religious Function of the Psyche</u>, pp. 110-111, Routledge, New York, 1996.

[56] Ibid., p. 112. Seen from this view when emotional difficulties are being experienced it's the Self attempting to provide an opportunity to the individual to gain more Self-consciousness.

[57] The Hero With A Thousand Faces, Bollingen Series XVII, Princeton University Press, Third Printing 1973.

[58] See Lionel Corbett's book The Religious Function of the psyche, Routledge, New York, 1996.

[59] Matthew 11: 11, Ibid

[60] Matthew 12: 11-12, Ibid

[61] John 10:34-36, Catholic Study Bible

[62] New Revised Standard Version, The Complete Parallel Bible

[63] Matthew 5: 14a, 16. Lamsa Translation

[64] John 14: 12, Ibid

[65] Acts 17: 28, Holy Bible: The New Scofield Reference Bible

[66] Matthew 13: 24; Matt 13: 31-32; Matt 13: 44, The Catholic Study Bible

[67] Matthew 13: 45-46, Ibid

[68] Ibid

[69] P. 37, Jung, Aion

[70] Mark 9:38-41, The Catholic Study Bible

[71] Edward Schillebeechx, JESUS An Experiment in Christology, p. the Foreword, Crossroad Publishing Company, New York, 1981

[72] P. 594, The Academy for Future Science, 3rd edition, 1987

[73] Romans 8: 18b-19; Col 1: 27b, Lamsa translation

[74] Eph 4: 17-24, New Revised Standard Version, Complete Parallel Bible

[75] Phil 2:5-7, The New Scofield Reference Bible

[76] 1 Cor 10: 1-4. The Catholic Study Bible

[77] Romans 8: 1-4, 9-11, 14-23, 27-31, 35a, 38-39, New Scofield Reference Bible

[78] 1 Cor 2: 6-7, 12, 15-16, Ibid

[79] Jung, Aion, P. 68-69.

[80] 1 Cor 12:27, The Catholic Study Bible

[81] 1 Cor 15:20-28, 51-54,   The New Scofield Reference Bible

[82] 2 Cor 5:17-21, Ibid

[83] Eph 2:10, New Jerusalem Bible, (Biblical text copyright © 1985 by Darton, Longman & Todd Ltd and Doubleday, a division of Bantam Doubleday Dell Publishing Group, Inc.) The Complete Parallel Bible

[84] Col 1: 24-27, New American Bible, (the New American Bible with Revised Psalms and Revised New Testament, copyright © 1986, 1991 by the Confraternity of Christian Doctrine, 3211 Fourth Street, N.E., Washington, D.C. 20017.) The Complete Parallel Bible

[85] Col 3: 8-11, New Revised Standard Version, The Complete Parallel Bible

[86] Catholic Study Bible

[87] Gal 3:24-29; 4:1-7, The New Scofield Reference Bible

[88] Gal 5:1, 13-14, Ibid

[89] Gal. 2:20, Ibid

[90] P. 1266, Ibid
[91] The Catholic Study Bible
[92] The New Scofield Reference Bible
[93] The Catholic Study Bible
[94] Both from The New Scofield Reference Bible
[95] Donald Curtis, <u>Finding the Christ</u>, p. 11-23, CSA Press, 1977.
[96] P. 79, <u>The Coming of the Cosmic Christ</u>: The Healing of Mother Earth and the Birth of a Global Renaissance, Harper San Francisco, 1988.

Chapter 3
[97] 3 Nephi 28:10, <u>The Book of Mormon, Another Testament of Jesus Christ</u>. The Church of Jesus Christ of Latter Day Saints, 1987.
[98] Section 88: 13, <u>Doctrines and Covenants</u>, The Church of Jesus Christ of Latter Day Saints, 1986
[99] Section 88: 6, Doctrines and Covenant
[100] Section 88: 7-12, Doctrines and Covenants
[101] 93:38, Doctrine & Covenants
[102] 93:33, Ibid
[103] <u>The Field: The Quest For The Secret Force of the Universe</u>, p. XIII- XIV, Harper Collins Publishers Inc, New York, 2002
[104] Verse 132: 37, Doctrine & Covenants
[105] Section 76: 50-51, 55-56, 58-59, Ibid
[106] P. 183, Edited by Andrew Harvey, Shambhala Boston/London, 1998

Chapter 4
[107] Erich Fromm. <u>You Shall Be As Gods</u>. P. 71, Ballantine Books, 1983.
[108] Ibid, 98
[109] Ibid, p. 98
[110] P. 98-99, You Shall Be As Gods.
[111] John 5: 30, The Catholic Study Bible
[112] P. 97, You Shall Be As Gods
[113] Ibid, p. 110
[114] Ibid, p. 111
[115] Ibid, p. 111
[116] Matthew 18" 19-20, The Catholic Study Bible
[117] Matthew 28: 20, The Catholic Study bible
[118] P. 118, You Shall Be As Gods
[119] Ibid, P. 119
[120] <u>Teachings of the Christian Mystics</u>, p, xxxvi, Edited by Andrew Harvey, Shambhala 1998

[121] See Matthew Fox' Original Blessing, particularly Appendix B for the details of the Fall/Redemption and Creation-Centered Spiritualities at a Glance, pp. 316-319, Bear & Company, Santa Fe, New Mexico, 1983.

[122] Romans 8: 28, Catholic Study Bible

[123] See website: **www.archives.gov/education/lessons/fdr-inaugural/images/address-2.gif**; & -3.gif

[124] The Urantia Book, P. 1889, 8th Printing, 1984, Urantia Foundation, Chicago

[125] Ibid, p. 1890.

[126] Quote by Webster Tarpley. See full article entitled *30 Million Productive Jobs to Rebuild US Infrastructure, Industry and Agriculture: The Program to End the Economic Depression* at www.tarpley.net

[127] From the Science of Christian Economy, and other prison writings, p. 94, Schiller Institute, Washington, D.C., 1991

[128] Teachings of the Christian Mystics, p. xxii – xxiii.

[129] JESUS: An Experiment in Christology, p.244, Crossroad Publishing Company, New York, 1981

[130] Reference here is made to Lionel Corbett's, The Religious Function of the Psyche, Chapter 9, *SIN AND EVIL - A psychological approach,* Routledge, New York, 1996.

[131] Ibid, p. 196.

[132] The American Heritage Dictionary, 2nd College Ed., Houghton Mifflin, 1982.

[133] Proclus' 13th Proposition: from the Course Reading Material provided by University Philosophical Research for Dr. Pierre Grimes' *The Wisdom of Classical Philosophy* Course, which uses the Barbara Stecker translation.

[134] Teachings of the Christian Mystics, p. 50-51, Edited by Archer Harvey, Shambhala Books, 1998.

[135] Taken from the Course Reading Material Notebook.

[136] The American Heritage Dictionary, 2nd College Ed.

[137] Refer to Pierre Hadot, What is Ancient Philosophy?, p. 238, Harvard Press, 2002.

[138] Taken from *On Beryllus,* p. 303-4, which is in Toward a New Council of Florence "On the Peace of Faith & Other Works by Nicolaus of Cusa, Translated by William F. Wertz Jr., Schiller Institute, 1995.

[139] *Timaeus*, 29a. Plato: Complete Works, p. 1235, John M. Cooper, Editor, Hackett Publishing, 1997

[140] Proclus' 148 Proposition as cited in the Course Reading Material Notebook from UPR..

[141] P. 472, in Toward a New Council of Florence "On the Peace of Faith & Other Works by Nicolaus of Cusa, Translated by William F. Wertz Jr., Schiller Institute, 1995.

[142] Dr. Pierre Grimes, audio-lecture Tape 10 for his *The Wisdom of Classical Philosophy* Course, UPR.

[143] Plato: Complete Works, p.990, Edited by John M. Copper, Hackett Publishing, 1997

[144] Synergetics: Explorations in the Geometry of Thinking, 1975, p. 4-9, MacMillan Publishing Co., Inc, New York

[145] Critical Path, , p. xxiii-xxv, 1981.

[146] The Farther Reaches of Human Nature, p. 256, An Esalen Book, Viking Press, New York, 1971.

[147] Reference to Lyndon Larouche's book Earth's Next Fifty Years, (and that as U.S. President FDR's Bretton woods monetary system and other 1933-1945 U.S. reforms typified) LaRouche PAC, Leesburg, Virginia, 2005

[148] See Larouchepac.com for full details of this building the future policy and project.

About the Author

Julian Bruno received his Bachelor of Art Degree from Lamar University in Beaumont, Texas in 1986.

In the 1990's he "discovered" the writings of Edmond Bordeaux Szekely, published by the Biogenic Society, on the Essenes, such as The Essene Gospel of Peace and From Enoch to the Dead Sea Scrolls, which cited Enoch as the founder of the Essenes. Being inspired by the character of Enoch from these writings and from the Book of Genesis, Julian gave himself the middle name of Enoch, since he didn't have a middle name and wanted one. Julian Enoch Bruno received his Master of Arts Degree in Consciousness Studies from the University of Philosophical Research, located in Los Angeles in 2003.

Julian also is the Production Manager for a medical device company called Lifestream Purification Systems, LLC, in Austin, Texas, which produces the Angel of Water®. Julian resonates with the words of Alexander Hamilton in his *Report on the Subject of Manufactures* (1791), which reads, "*To cherish and stimulate the activity of the human mind, by multiplying the objects of enterprise, is not among the least considerable of the expedients, by which the wealth of a nation may be promoted.*"